INCOME TAX ACT- SUPREME COURT'S LEADING CASE LAWS

CASE NOTES- FACTS- FINDINGS OF APEX COURT JUDGES & CITATIONS

JAYPRAKASH BANSILAL SOMANI

ISBN 979-888555205-9

Dedicated

To

All the Past & Present Judges of the Supreme Court of India.

Salute to their wisdom.

Salute to their interpretation of Law.

Salute to their elaborative judgement writing.

Contents

Contents

Preface

Dear Learned Advocates of the Income Tax Tribunals, Appellate Tribunals, High Courts, Supreme Court, Chartered Accountants, Tax Practitioners, Corporates & Individuals

I am very delighted to provide you a book on 'INCOME TAX ACT'- Supreme Court's Leading Case Laws'.

In this book you will get...

1. Name of the Case i. e. Cause title

2.Relevant Sections discussed in the case

3. Hon'ble Judges/Coram of the case

4.Number of PDF Pages in Original Judgement of the case

5. All available Citations of the case

6. Case Note with appeal allowed/ dismissed or disposed off

7. Facts of the case

8. Hon'ble Apex Court's findings, while dismissing/allowing or disposing the appeal

9. Ratio Decidendi if any.

My special thanks to Manupatra, because of their web portal I can compile this book in well manner. I am also thankful to Notion Press to support me to publish & market this book throughout the Country. Thanks to my Juniors, Advocate Colleagues & Insolvency Professional Colleagues to support me in this venture.

Mr Rachit Manchanda has helped me a lot to compile this book.

I hope this book will add some value addition in the wealth of your legal knowledge. Your positive feedbacks will boost me to compile/ write further books & negative feedbacks will improve my skills. Kindly send your valuable feedbacks by email.

Thanks with Regards,

Jayprakash B. Somani

Advocate, Supreme Court of India

Email: jaysomani64@gmail.com

Web Site: www.jayprakashsomani.com

Call: 9322188701, 8384051134, 9318381287

Acknowledgements

Printed & Published by
Notion Press
No. 8, 3rd Cross Street,
CIT Colony, Mylapore,
Chennai, Tamil Nadu- 600004

♡♡♡

Managed by
Jayprakash Somani Advocates & Solicitors
Law Firm for Supreme Court of India
Delhi Office
257 C, Pocket 1, Mayur Vihar Phase 1, Delhi 110091.
Call 8384051134, 9322188701, 8459194576, 9318381287 01141051516
Supreme Court Chamber
312, 3rd Floor, M. C. Setalvad Block, In front of 'D' Gate, Bhagwan Das Road, Supreme Court of India, New Delhi 110001
Contact: 8459194576, 9811011747,
www.jayprakashsomani.com

♡♡♡

Books are available online at
1. **Notion Press:** https://notionpress.com/author/jayprakash_somani
2. **Amazon:** https://www.amazon.in/s?k=jayprakash+somani
3. **Flipkart:** https://www.flipkart.com/search?q=Jayprakash%20Somani

♡♡♡

ONE

Commissioner of Income Tax, Delhi (Central) Vs.Singh Engineering Works P. Ltd., 1969

Hon'ble Judges/Coram: A.N. Grover, J.C. Shah and K.S. Hegde, JJ.

Relevant Section:

INCOME-TAX ACT, 1961 - Section 297(2)(g)

MANU/SC/0231/1970

Equivalent Citation: AIR1971SC95, [1970]78ITR90(SC), (1970)2SCC428, [1971]1SCR769

No. of pages in the original judgement: 2

Case Note:

Direct Taxation - saving of proceedings - Sections 18 A (2) and 18 A (9) of Income Tax Act, 1922 and Sections 273 and 279 (2) of Income Tax (Amendment) Act, 1961 - new Income Tax Act came into force from first day of April 1962 - assessing officer had stared proceedings for default in payment of advance tax under relevant provisions of old Act (for assessment year in which new Act came into force) - Tribunal was of opinion that new Act does not save proceedings in old Act - whether proceedings initiated under old Act can be continued under relevant provisions of new Act - any proceedings for imposition of penalty of any assessment year ending on 31.03.1962 or any earlier year which is completed on or after 01.04.1962 may be initiated and penalty can be imposed under new Act - assessment proceedings for assessment year in which new Act came into force shall be initiated under relevant provisions of new Act - penalty shall also be imposed as per new Ac

Brief facts of the case:

The respondent company which is an assessee was required by the Income tax Officer by notices issued under Section 18A(1) of the Indian Income tax Act 1922, hereinafter called the "Old Act" to make an advance payment of tax amounting to Rs. 3,17,077 for the assessment year 1960-61 and Rs. 3,54,911 for the assessment year 1961-62. The assessee chose to file its own estimate of tax under Section 18A(2) and in accordance therewith it paid two installments of advance tax of Rs. 38,333/- each for the assessment year 1960-61 and three installments of Rs. 12,875/-each for the assessment year 1961-62. Thereafter the assessee filed revised estimates of tax in the month of March 1960 and March 1961 respectively estimating the tax at Rs. 1,80,000/- for each of the assessment years on a total income of Rs. 4 lakhs. The balance of advance tax as per its revised estimate was paid in time after deducting the installments which had already been paid. The assessee subsequently riled its returns of income for the aforesaid two years declaring the total income of Rs. 4,53,942/- and Rs. 7,02,383/- respectively. The Income tax Officer completed the assessment of total income of Rs. 5,35,000/- and Rs. 8,99,029/- for the assessment years 1960-61 and 1961-62 on January 21, 1963 after the Income tax Act 1961, hereinafter called the "New Act" had come into force. The Income tax Officer took the view that the assessee had furnished inaccurate and untrue estimates of tax and had not given any satisfactory explanation in respect of them. He imposed penalties under Section 273 of the new Act amounting to Rs. 13,700/- and Rs. 12,342/. for the assessment years 1960-61 and 1961-62 respectively. Appeals to the Appellate Assistant Commissioner in the matter of imposition of penalty were rejected. The Appellate Tribunal held that the penalties could not have been imposed under the provisions of Section 273 of the new Act in respect of the two assessment years in question. It was said inter alia, that in the absence of any deeming provision in the new Act the default under Section 18A of the old Act could not be treated as a default under Section 212 of the new Act and that Section 297(2)(g) of the new Act did not save the proceedings under Section 18A of the old Act. A question of law was referred directly to this Court under the provisions of Section 257 of the new Act owing to the conflict between the decisions of the various High Courts.

Held,

We are further unable to agree that the language to Section 271 does not warrant the taking of proceedings under that section when a default has been committed by failure to comply with a notice issued under Section 22(2) of the Act of 1922. It is true that Clause (a) of Sub-section (1) of Section 271 mentions the corresponding provisions of the Act of 1961 but that will not make the part relating to payment of penalty inapplicable once it is held that Section 297(2)(g) governs the case. Both Sections 271(1) and 297(2)(g) have to be read together and in harmony and so read the only conclusion possible is that for the imposition of a penalty in respect of any assessment for the year ending on March 31, 1962 or any earlier year which is completed after first day of April 1962 the proceedings have to be initiated and the penalty imposed in accordance with the provisions of Section 271 of the Act of 1961. Thus the assessee would be liable to a penalty as provided by Section 271(1) for the default mentioned in Section 28(1) of the Act of 1922 if his case falls within the terms of Section 297(2)(g). We may usefully refer to this Court's decision in Third Income tax Officer, Mangalore v. Damodar Bhat MANU/SC/0099/1968 : [1969]71ITR806(SC) with reference to Section 297(2)(j) of the Act of 1961. According to it in a case falling within that section in a proceeding for recovery of tax and penalty imposed under the Act of 1922 it is not required that all the sections of the new Act relating to recovery or collection should be literally applied but only such of the sections will apply as are appropriate in the particular case and subject, if necessary, to suitable modifications. In other words, the procedure of the new Act will apply to cases contemplated by Section 297(2)(j) of the new Act mutatis mutandis. Similarly the provision of Section 271 of the Act of 1961 will apply mutatis mutandis to proceedings relating to penalty initiated in accordance with Section 297(2)(g) of that Act.

In our judgment Section 297(2)(g) is clearly applicable to the present case inasmuch as the assessment was completed on or after the first day of April 1962. The provisions of the new Act contained in Section 273 will apply mutatis mutandis to proceedings relating to penalty initiated in accordance with Section 297(2)(g) of the new Act. The question which has been referred to us is answered in the affirmative and in favour of the Commissioner of Income tax who will be entitled to his costs in this Court.

TWO

SOUTHERN TECHNOLOGIES LTD. VS. JOINT COMMNR. OF INCOME TAX, COIMBATORE, 2010

Hon'ble Judges/Coram: S.H. Kapadia and Aftab Alam, JJ.

Relevant Section:

Income-Tax Act, 1961 - Section 043D, Income-Tax Act, 1961 - Section 37, Income-Tax Act, 1961 - Section 36(viia), Income-Tax Act, 1961 - Section 36(1)(Vii), Income-Tax Act, 1961 - Section 2(24)

Equivalent Citation: I(2010)BC625, I(2010)BC625(SC), [2010]153CompCas674(SC), (2010)1CompLJ577(SC), (2010)1CompLJ577(SC), (2010)228CTR(SC)440, [2010]320ITR577(SC), JT2010(1)SC14, 2010(1)SCALE329, (2010)2SCC548, [2010]2SCR380, [2010]187TAXMAN346(SC), 2010(1)UJ387, MANU/SC/0023/2010

No. of pages in the original judgement: 25

Case Note:

Direct Taxation - Non Performing Assets(NPA) - Deduction – Claim thereof - Sections 2(24), 28 and 37 of the Income Tax Act 1961 -Assessee (NBFC"s) claimed deduction under Section 36(1)(vii) in terms of RBI Directions 1998 on the ground that Assessee had to debit the said amount to P&L Account reducing its Profits, contending it to be write off, also contended that there has been diminution in the value of its assets for which Assessee was entitled to deduction under Section 37as a trading loss - Tribunal allowed the claim of the Assessee subsequently rejected by the High Court in appeal - Hence this Appeal - Held, Section 45JA of the RBI Act stipulates anticipated loss to be taken into account but expected income to be taken note of - Section 37 applies to items which do not fall under Section 30 to 36 - If provision doubtful debt expressly excluded from Section 36(1)(vii) then such apro vision cannot claim deduction under Section 37 - NPA under commercial accounting is not "income" hence on the basis of "Real Income Theory" it cannot be added back - Provision for doubtful debts not allowable and NPA since a doubtful debt, not allowable under Section 37(1) - RBI Directions 1998 and the Income Tax Act operate in different fields and RBI Directions cannot override the Income TaxAct,1961 - Appeal Dismissed

Brief facts of the case:

At the outset, it may be stated that categorization of assets into doubtful, sub-standard and loss is not in dispute.

The financial year of the Appellant is July to June and the P&L Account and the Balance Sheet are drawn as on 30th June. The P&L Account and Balance Sheet is for shareholders, Reserve Bank of India (RBI) and Registrar of Companies (ROC) under the Companies Act, 1956. However, for IT Act, a separate P&L Account is made out for the year ending 31st March and the Balance Sheet as on that date is prepared and submitted to the Assessing Officer(AO) for computing the Total Income under the IT Act, which is not for use of RBI or ROC.

For the accounting year ending 31.03.1998, Assessee debited Rs. 81,68,516/- as Provision against NPA in the P&L Account on three counts, viz., Hire-Purchase of Rs. 57,38,980/-, Bill Discounting of Rs. 12,79,500/- and Loans and Advances of Rs. 31,84,701/-, in all, totalling Rs. 1,02,03,121/- from which AO allowed deduction of Rs. 20,34,605/- on account of Hire Purchase Finance Charges leaving a balance provision for NPA of Rs. 81,68,516/-.

Held,

In the case of **State of Madras v. V.G. Row**MANU/SC/0013/1952 : 1952 SCR 597 this Court observed as follows:

It is important in this context to bear in mind that the test of reasonableness, wherever prescribed, should be applied to each individual statute impugned, and no abstract standard, or general pattern of reasonableness can be laid down as applicable to all cases. The nature of the right alleged to have been infringed, the underlying purpose of the restrictions imposed, the extent and urgency of the evil sought to be remedied thereby, the disproportion of the imposition, the prevailing conditions at the time, should all enter into the judicial verdict.

In the case of **Barclays Mercantile Business Finance Ltd. v. Mawson (Inspector of Taxes)** 2005 (1) All ER 97 the House of Lords observed that "a tax is generally imposed by reference to economic activities or transactions which exist in the real world". When an economic activity is to be valued, it is open to the law makers to take into account various factors like public investments, disclosure and transparency in the matter of maintenance of accounts, reflection of true and correct profits, etc. This is precisely what is done by RBI Directions 1998.

For the afore-stated reasons, we find no merit in the civil Appeals filed by the NBFCs, so also in the Transferred Cases, and, accordingly, the same are dismissed with no order as to costs

THREE

Commissioner of Income Tax Vs. Sercon Pvt. Ltd., 1997

Relevant Section: INCOME-TAX ACT, 1961 - Section 261

Equivalent Citation: [1998]229ITR120(SC), MANU/SC/2182/1997

No. of pages in the original judgement: 2

Case Note:

In all income-tax and allied tax matters, it is essential for the appellant or the petitioner to file the order rendered by the Appellate Tribunal in the appeal and also the statement of the case in cases where such a statement of the case is drawn up, therefore, time granted to the revenue to produce the relevant document within four weeks.

Brief facts of the Case:

The Income-tax Appellate Tribunal referred the following question of law for the decision of the High Court of Gujarat (see MANU/GJ/0037/1981 : [1982]136ITR881(Guj) : [1982]136ITR881(Guj)) :

"Whether the Tribunal was justified in law in holding that the land in question bearing final Plot No. 522-C sold by the assessee was not agricultural land and that the excess of Rs. 10,65,243 was liable to be taxed as capital gains even when the plot in question at the time of its sale was entered in the Government revenue records as agricultural land ?"

It is evident that the Appellate Tribunal held that the land in question is not agricultural land. But the High Court has taken a different view and has held that the Tribunal erred in holding that the land sold by the assessee - the subject-matter of this proceeding - is not agricultural land.

Held,

Counsel for the Revenue prays for time to file the order of the Appellate Tribunal and also the statement of the case. The appeal was filed nearly 13 years ago and the Revenue had sufficient time to file these documents. Why the Revenue has not so far filed these documents, which should be referred to at the time of hearing, is not clear. In any view of the matter, we are not inclined to dismiss the appeal on this technical ground. We grant time to the Revenue to produce the relevant documents within four weeks. List the matter after four weeks.

The Registrar General will take note of the directions given hereinabove and direct the Registry to see that the above orders are procured by the Registry in all cases coming under reference jurisdiction in tax matters.

FOUR

Gujarat Travancore Agency, Cochin Vs. Commissioner of Income Tax, Kerala, Ernakulam 1989

Hon'ble Judges/Coram: R.S. Pathak, C.J. and M.H. Kania, J.

Relevant Section: INCOME-TAX ACT, 1961 - Section 276C, INCOME-TAX ACT, 1961 - Section 271(1)(a), INCOME-TAX ACT, 1961 - Section 139(1)

Equivalent Citation: AIR1989SC1671, (1989)77CTR(SC)174, 1989(42)ELT350(S.C.), [1989]177ITR455(SC), JT1989(2)SC446, 1989(2)KLT1(SC), 1989(1)SCALE1275, (1989)3SCC52, [1989]2SCR1000, [1989]44TAXMAN278(SC), MANU/SC/0332/1989

No. of pages in the original judgement : 2

Case note:

Unless there is something in the language of the statute indicating the need to establish the element of mens rea it is generally sufficient to prove that a default in complying with the statute has occurred. There is nothing in s. 271(1)(a) which required that means rea must be proved before penalty can be levied under that provisions.

Brief facts of the case:

These appeals, by certificate granted by the High Court of Kerala, are directed against the judgment of that High Court answering the following question of law referred to it in an Income-tax Reference in favour of the Revenue and against the assessee:

Whether, on the facts and in the circumstances of the case, the Tribunal is justified in law in cancelling the penalties levied under Section 271(1)(a) of the Income-tax Act, 1961, for the assessment years 1965-66 -and 1966-67 ?

The assessee is a registered firm trading in hill produce. The assessee did not file its income-tax return under the Income-tax Act, 1961 for the assessment year 1965-66 Within the statutory period, that is to say by 30th June, 1965, and instead applied for time to file the return. Time was granted Up to 31st August, 1966. Yet no return was filed. It was only after notice under Section 139(2) of the Act was served on the assessee on 22nd September, 1967 that it. filed a return on the next day. Similarly for the assessment year 1966-67 no return was filed up to 30th June, 1966. No application for extension of time was made either. When notice under Section 139(2) was served on the assessee on 21st June, 1966 it filed a return on 23rd September, 1967. In the circumstances, the Income-tax Officer initiated penalty proceedings against the assessee under Section 271(1)(a) of the Act for the two assessment years. A sum of Rs. 14,784/- was levied as penalty for the assessment year 1965-66 and a sum of Rs. 11,447/- was imposed as penalty for the assessment year 1966-67. The explanation of the assessee that he was under the bona fide belief that he had no assessable income and had, therefore, not filed the returns earlier was not accepted by the Income-tax Officer. In appeal before the Appellate Assistant Commissioner of Income-tax, the assessee did not press the ground that there was no deliberate omission on his part to file the returns and that therefore Section 271(1)(a) of the Act was not attracted. In second appeal before the Income-tax Appellate Tribunal permission was granted to the assessee to raise the ground. The Appellate Tribunal allowed the appeals holding that the Income-tax Officer had failed to bring on record any material to show that the explanation of the assessee tendered before him in regard to the delay should not be accepted, and that as the element of mens rea was required to be proved and had not been proved, the penalties were liable to be cancelled.

Held,

In most cases of criminal liability, the intention of the Legislature is that the penalty should serve as a deterrent. The creation of an offence by Statute proceeds on the assumption that society suffers injury by the act or omission of the defaulter and that a deterrent must be imposed to discourage the repetition of the offence. In the case of a proceeding under

Section 271(1)(a), however, it seems that the intention of the legislature is to emphasise the fact of loss of Revenue and to provide a remedy for such loss, although no doubt an element of coercion is present in the penalty. In this connection the terms in which the penalty falls to be measured is significant. Unless there is something in the language of the statute indicating the need to establish the element of mens rea it is generally sufficient to prove that a default in complying with the statute has occurred. In our opinion, there is nothing in Section 271(l)(a) which requires that mens rea must be proved before penalty can be levied under that provision.<mpara>

We are supported by the statement in Corpus Juris Secundum, Volume 85, page 580, paragraph 1023:

A penalty imposed for a tax delinquency is a civil obligation, remedial and coercive in its nature, and is far different from the penalty for a crime or a fine or forfeiture provided as punishment for the violation of criminal or penal laws.

Accordingly, we hold that the element of mens rea was not required to be proved in the proceedings taken by the Income-tax Officer under Section 271(1)(a) of the Income-tax Act against the assessee for the assessment years 1965-66 and 1966-67.

In the result the appeals fail and are dismissed with costs.

FIVE

Broach Distt. Co-operative Cotton Sales Ginning and Pressing Society Limited Vs. Commissioner of Income Tax, Ahmedabad 1989

Hon'ble Judges/Coram: R.S. Pathak, C.J. and M.H. Kania, J.

Relevant Section: INCOME-TAX ACT, 1961 - Section 81

Equivalent Citation: AIR1989SC1493, (1989)2CompLJ164(SC), (1989)2CompLJ164(SC), (1989)2CompLJ164(SC), (1989)77CTR(SC)70, (1989)2GLR1336, [1989]177ITR418(SC), JT1989(2)SC267, 1989(1)SCALE1138, (1989)2SCC679, [1989]2SCR720, [1989]44TAXMAN439(SC), 1989(2)UJ150, MANU/SC/0084/1989

No. of pages in the original judgement: 3

Case Note:

Direct Taxation - exemption - Section 81 of Income Tax Act, 1961 - whether income of co-operative society from ginning and pressing exempted under Section 81 (1) (c) - Section 81 (1) (c) exempted profits and gain of co-operative societies from marketing of agricultural produce of its members - High Court held ginning and pressing of cotton with aid of power though incidental to marketing activity not exempted under Section 81 (1) (c) - ginning and pressing of cotton part of integral process of marketing - activity incidental or ancillary to marketing of produce of members - income exempted under Section 81 (1) (c).

Brief facts of the case:

Those appeals by certificate granted by the High Court of Gujarat are directed against the judgment of the High Court answering the following question in favour of the Revenue and against the assessee : -

Whether, on the facts and in the circumstances of the case, the income of the Society from ginning and pressing was exempt under Section 81(i)(c) of the Income-tax Act, 1961, as it stood prior to its amendment on 1st April, 1968?

The assessee is a co-operative society constituted under the Co-operative Societies Act. The objects of the society intend that it should press cotton and pack the bundles for its individual members as well as other customers, to use its machinery for any useful work of its members, and to sell raw cotton, cotton seeds and other agricultural products. The assessee possesses a ginning and pressing factory to cater to the needs of its members. It gets raw cotton from the members, and gins and presses the cotton for marketing on behalf of its members. For rendering the services of ginning and pressing before selling the goods, the assessee charges the members a certain amount by way of ginning and pressing charges. It also charges commission for the sale of the finished product.

Held,

An attempt was made by learned Counsel for the Revenue to raise the point that ginning and pressing into cotton bales changed the character of the cotton and therefore, what was marketed was not the agricultural produce of the members of the assessee. This point was not raised at any earlier stage by the Revenue and cannot be permitted to be taken now.

We are of opinion that the assessee is entitled to the exemption of the profits and gains derived from the activity of the entire business of ginning and pressing of cotton and marketing it by virtue of Clause (c)of Section

81(i) of the Income-tax Act, and that the High Court erred in holding to the contrary.

In the result the appeals are allowed and the question referred by the Income-tax Appellate Tribunal to the High Court must be answered in the affirmative, in favour of the assessee and against the Revenue. The assessee is entitled to its costs.

SIX

SWADESHI COTTON MILLS CO. LTD. VS. COMMISSIONER OF INCOME TAX, UTTAR PRADESH (NO. 2), 1966

Hon'ble Judges/Coram: J.C. Shah, Vashishtha Bhargava and Vaidynathier Ramaswami, JJ.

Relevant Section:

INDIAN INCOME-TAX ACT, 1922 - Section 10(2)

Equivalent Citation: [1967]63ITR65(SC), MANU/SC/0157/1966

No. of pages in the original judgement: 2

Case Note:

Direct Taxation - capital expenditure - Section 10 (2) of Income Tax Act, 1922 - whether payment of compensatory amount has been rightly disallowed as capital expenditure within meaning of Section 10 (2) (xv) - in present case amount paid was in respect of breach of contracts in regard to purchase of textile machinery which would have been a capital asset - payment was made to avoid larger capital expenditure that would not have served interests of appellant-company - payment was not made to earn profits for purpose of carrying on business from day to day and allowable to be deducted as capital expenditure.

Brief facts of the case:

The appellant is a public limited company carrying on the business manufacturing and selling cloth and other textile goods. During the previous year ending on 31st December, 1948, corresponding to the assessment year 1949-50, the appellant entered into two contracts with two other parties for purchase of textile machinery in order to expand its factory. Subsequently, the appellant-company, having regard to altered circumstances, decided to cancel both the contracts as, in its opinion, the machinery to be purchased would not be required for its business. On cancellation of these contracts, the appellant had to pay a sum of Rs. 15,000 as compensation to one of the contracting parties and Rs. 20,000 to the other contracting party who demanded compensation for breach of contract. The appellant claimed that these amounts were paid in the interest of its business as, otherwise, the appellant would have had to track very costly machinery which would not have served any useful purpose, so that this was an expenditure incurred by the company wholly and exclusively for the purpose of its business. The deduction thus claimed under section 10(2)(xv) of the Income-tax Act was, however, disallowed by the Income-tax Officer, and that order was upheld by the Appellate Assistant Commissioner and the Income-tax Appellate Tribunal. Thereupon, on an application under section 66(1) of the Income-tax Act, the Tribunal referred the following question for the opinion of the High Court at Allahabad :

"Whether, on the facts of the case, the payment of compensation amounting to Rs. 35,000 has been rightly disallowed as capital expenditure within the meaning of section 10(2)(xv) of the Income-tax Act, 1922 ?"

The High Court answered the question against the appellant and upheld the order of the Tribunal. Consequently, the appellant and upheld the order of the Tribunal. Consequently, the appellant has come up to this court in this appeal by special leave.

Held,

On the facts put forward by the appellant itself and accepted by the Tribunal and the High Court, it is clear that the sum of Rs. 35,000 claimed as deduction under section 10(2)(xv) was really paid for breach of contracts in respect of purchase of textile machinery which would have been a capital asset. The payment was, therefore made to avoid a larger capital expenditure that would not have served the interests of the appellant-company. Such a payment made is clearly in the nature of a capital expenditure and not an expenditure incurred wholly or exclusively for the purpose of the business. The payment was neither made for the purpose of earning profits, nor for the purpose of furthering, protecting or continuing its business which was to be carried on from day to day. The payment was made with the object of avoiding an unnecessary investment in capital assets, and was an amount which was altogether outside the account of profits and gains, in the computation of which deductions are allowable for expenditure incurred wholly and exclusive for earning those profits and gains. It is, therefore, clear that this amount could not have been claimed has a legitimate deduction under section 10(2)(xv) of the Income-tax Act. Our view is supported by the observations of Rowlatt J. in "Countess Warwick" Steamship Co. Ltd. v. Ogg. The appeal consequently has no force and is dismissed with costs.

Appeal dismissed.

SEVEN

COMMISSIONER OF INCOME TAX VS. SHRI ARBUDA MILLS LTD., 1996

Hon'ble Judges/Coram:J Verma, S Bharucha, S V Manohar

Relevant Section:

INCOME-TAX ACT, 1961 - Section 263

Equivalent Citation: (1998)147CTR(SC)474, MANU/SC/2183/1996

No. of pages in the original judgement: 2

Case Note:

Direct Taxation - Merger of Assessment - Section 257 of Income Tax Act, 1961- Whether order of assessment passed by ITO under Section 143(3) read with Section 144 B on 31st July, 1978, had merged with that of CIT (A) dt. 15th December, 1979, in respect of three items in dispute so as to exclude jurisdiction of CIT under Section 263? - Held, amendment made in Section 263 of Act by Finance Act, 1989, with retrospective effect from 1st June, 1988 - Consequence of the said amendment made with retrospective effect is that the powers under Section 263 of CIT shall extend and shall be deemed always to have extended to such matters as had not been considered and decided in an appeal - Accordingly, even in respect of aforesaid three items, powers of the CIT under Section 263 shall extend and shall be deemed always to have extended to them because the same had not been considered and decided in appeal filed by assessee - Question referred is, therefore, answered in negative, in favour of Revenue and against assessee.

Brief facts of the case:

he Tribunal has referred under s. 257 of the IT Act, 1961, the following question of law for decision of this Court, namely :

"Whether, on the facts and in the circumstances of the case, the order of assessment passed by the ITO under s. 143(3) r/w s. 144B on 31st July, 1978, had merged with that of the CIT (A) dt. 15th December, 1979, in respect of the three items in dispute so as to exclude the jurisdiction of the CIT under s. 263 ?"

The assessee is a company. The relevant assessment year is 1975-76 ending on 31st December, 1974. The assessment was completed under s. 143(3) r/w s. 144B, on 31st March, 1978, in which the net business loss was computed at Rs. 3,61,086 and the income under the head "Capital gains" at Rs. 38,874. The ITO had made certain additions and disallowance while computing the loss and income as above and had also accepted, inter alia, the following three claims :

(i) Deduction of a sum of Rs. 23,82,621 by way of provision for gratuity;

(ii) Depreciation on Rs. 4,21,000 which was paid by the assessee to United Textile Industries as consideration for transfer of installed property of 17,480 spindles and 400 looms of Old Manek Chowk Mills;

(iii) Loss on account of difference in exchange rate which was referable to the purchase of machinery, etc., as revenue expenditure.

Held,

For the removal of doubts, it is hereby declared that, for the purposes of this sub-section, - where any order referred to in this sub-section and passed by the AO had been the subject-matter of any appeal filed on or before or after 1st June, 1988, the powers of the CIT under this sub-section shall extend and shall be deemed always to have extended to such matters as had not been considered and decided in such appeal".

The consequence of the said amendment made with retrospective effect is that the powers under s. 263 of the CIT shall extend and shall be deemed always to have extended to such matters as had not been considered and decided in an appeal. Accordingly, even in respect of the aforesaid three items, the powers of the CIT under s. 263 shall extend and shall be deemed always to have extended to them because the same had not been considered and decided in the appeal filed by the assessee. This is sufficient to answer the question which has been referred.

The question referred is, therefore, answered in the negative, in favour of the Revenue and against the assessee.

EIGHT

Jamnaprasad Kanhaiyalal Vs. Commissioner of Income Tax, M.P., Bhopal, 1981

Hon'ble Judges/Coram: A.N. Sen, E.S. Venkataramiah and R.S. Pathak, JJ.

Relevant Section:

INCOME-TAX ACT, 1961 - Section 68

Equivalent Citation: AIR1981SC1759, (1981)23CTR(SC)146, [1981]130ITR244(SC), (1981)3SCC441, [1981]3SCR849, MANU/SC/0304/1981

No. of pages in the original judgement: 5

Case Note:

Direct Taxation - disclosure - Section 24 of Finance Act, 1965, Section 68 of Income Tax Act, 1961 and Section 18 of Voluntary Disclosures Of Income and Wealth Act, 1976 - whether provisions of Section 24 can be construed as conferring any benefit, concession or immunity on any person other than person making declaration under provisions of Act - immunity under Section 24 was conferred on declarant only and there was nothing to preclude an investigation into true nature and source of credits - amount declared was to be charged to income tax as if such income were total income of declarant and it cannot be invoked in assessment proceedings relating to any person other than person making declaration under Act so as to rule out applicability of Section 68.

Brief facts of the case:

This is a direct reference under Section 257 of, the Income Tax Act, 1961 made by the Income Tax Appellate (Tribunal, Jabalpur, for short, The Appellate Tribunal), at the instance of the assessee. The reference is necessitated due to divergence of opinion, as reflected in the various decisions of different High Courts, with respect to the scope and effect of the Voluntary Disclosure Scheme under Section 24 of the Finance (No. 2) C Act, 1965 (the 'Act', for short).

The assessee, Messrs. Jamnaprasad Kanhaiyalal, is a partnership firm. The firm consists of 4 partners, namely, Kanhaiyalal and his 3 major sons, Rajkumar, Swatantrakumar and Santoshkumar with his minor son Satishkumar admitted to the benefits of the partnership. In the course of assessment proceedings for the assessment year 1967-68, the relevant accounting year of which was the year ending Diwali, 1966, the Income Tax Officer (ITO, for short) noticed in the books of account of the assessee five Cash credits of Rs. 9,250 each in the names of five sons of Kanhaiyalal, as detailed below :

		Rs.
Sailendrakumar	5 yrs.	9,250/-
Satishkumar	9 yrs.	9,250/-
Sunilkumar	7 yrs.	9,250/-
Swatantrakumar	16 yrs.	9,250/-
Santoshkumar	18 yrs.	9,250/-
		46,250/-

Held,

The acceptance of a disclosure statement made by a declarant under Section 24 of the Finance (No. 2) Act, 1965 cannot confer immunity on another person from tax liability in respect of the same sum of money. As was held by this Court in Ahmed Ibrahim S. Dhoraji v. The Commissioner of Wealth Tax Gujarat MANU/SC/0280/1981 : [1981]129ITR314(SC) . the liability imposed under Section 24 of the Finance (No. 2) Act, 1965 is identifiable with the income tax liability under the Income-tax Act. The scheme for voluntary disclosure of income and its taxation is only another mode provided by law for imposing income tax and recovering it. Consequently, the general principles which apply to assessments made under the Income-Tax Act would except for the provision to the contrary, be applicable to assessments made under Section 24 of the Finance (No. 2) Act, 1965. Accordingly, when the assessment to income tax is made under the latter enactment, it will be governed by the general principle that a finding recorded therein governs only the particular person assessed. The jurisdiction of an Income Tax Officer when making an assessment is concerned primarily with the issue whether the receipt under consideration constitutes the income of the assessee before him. Any finding reached by the Income Tax Officer touching a person not the assessee in the process of determining that issue cannot be regarded as an operative finding in favour of or against such person. The only exception to this rule centers on the limited class, and for the limited purpose, defined by this Court in Income-Tax Officer, A-Ward Sitapur v. Murudhar Bhagwan Das. MANU/SC/0097/1964 : [1964]52ITR335(SC) , 346. Viewed in the light of that principle it is apparent that the finality enacted by Sub-section (8) of Section 24 of the Finance (No. 2), Act, 1965 attaches to the assessment of the declarant only. It cannot in law operate in favour of or against any other person.

I am of opinion that the making of an assessment against a declarant on his disclosure statement under Section 24 of the Finance (No. 2) Act, 1965 cannot deprive an Income Tax Officer of jurisdiction to assess the same receipt in the hands of another person if, in a properly constituted assessment proceeding under the Income Tax Act, the receipt can be regarded as the taxable income of such other person. I would answer the first question in the affirmative, in favour of the Revenue and against the assessee. That being so, no answer is necessary to the second question. The Commissioner of Income-Tax is entitled to his costs of the reference

ppp

NINE

Rajasthan State Warehousing Corporation Vs. Commissioner of Income Tax, 2000

Hon'ble Judges/Coram: D.P. Wadhwa and S.S.M. Quadri, JJ.

Relevant Section:

INCOME-TAX ACT, 1961 - Section 37

Equivalent Citation: AIR2000SC972, (2000)159CTR(SC)132, [2000]242ITR450(SC), JT2000(2)SC373, 2000(2)SCALE44, (2000)3SCC126, [2000]1SCR1113, [2000]109TAXMAN145(SC), MANU/SC/0120/2000

No. of pages in the original judgement: 3

Case Note:

Income-tax - Exemption - Income-tax Officer allowed only expenditure as could be allocated to taxable income and disallowed rest of it which was referable to non-taxable income, being exempt under Section 10(29) of Act - On appeal, Commissioner accepted claim of Appellant that entire expenditure was deductible - Tribunal and High Court confirmed order of officer - Hence, this Appeal - Whether, business of Assessee being one and indivisible, Tribunal was right in holding that the expenses have to allocated in the same percentage as the different sources of income - Held, if exempted income and taxable income were earned from one and indivisible business then apportionment of expenditure could not be sustained - Therefore, income from various ventures was earned in course of one and indivisible business - Hence, impugned order upholding apportionment of expenditure and allowing deduction of only that proportion of it which was referable to taxable income, was unsustainable - Appeal allowed.

Ratio Decidendi:

"If exempted income and taxable income are earned from one and indivisible business then apportionment of expenditure cannot be sustained.

Brief facts of the case:

This appeal arises from the judgment and order of the Division Bench of the High Court of Judicature for Rajasthan Bench at Jaipur in Income-tax Reference No. 86 of 1987 dated November 9, 1993. The assessee is the appellant.

By the order under challenge the High Court answered the following question, referred to it under Section 256(1) of the Income-tax Act, 1961 (for short 'the Act'), in the affirmative, that is, in favour of the Revenue and against the assessee:

Whether on the facts and in the circumstances of the case and the business of the assessee being one and indivisible, the Tribunal was right in law in holding that the expenses have to allocated in the same percentage as the different sources of income and are not to be allowed in entirety as allowed by the Commissioner of Income-tax (A) after following decision noted in para 11 of the order dated 31.01.1985 for the assessment year 1974-75, 1975-76 and 1980-81?

Held,

Mr. Shukla has fairly conceded that if the exempted income and the taxable income are earned from one and indivisible business then the apportionment of the expenditure cannot be sustained. But, sub-limits the learned Counsel, in this case the "Tribunal did not record a finding that the business of the assessee is one indivisible, therefore, the apportionment of the expenditure is valid. We are afraid, we cannot accede to the contention of the learned Counsel inasmuch as a plain reading of the question itself shows that it embodies - "the business of the assessee being one and indivisible." This being the position, it is not open to the Revenue to contend that the business is not one and indivisible. In view of the fact that a perusal of the question itself discloses that income from various ventures is earned in the course of one and indivisible business, the impugned order upholding the apportionment of the expenditure and allowing deduction of only that proportion of it which is referable to taxable income, is unsustainable.

We, therefore, answer the question in the negative, that is, in favour of the assessee and against the Revenue. The order under appeal is accordingly set aside and the appeal is allowed with costs.

TEN

Commissioner of Income Tax, Bombay and Ors. Vs. Podar Cement Pvt. Ltd. and Ors.,1997

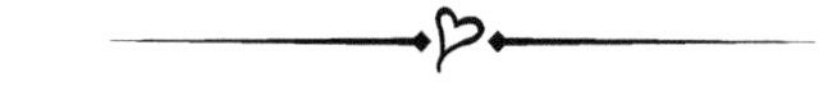

Hon'ble Judges/Coram: K.S. Paripoornan, K. Venkataswami and B.N. Kirpal, JJ.

Relevant Section:

Income-Tax Act, 1961 - Section 27, Income-Tax Act, 1961 - Section 22; Indian Income-Tax Act, 1922 - Section 9

Equivalent Citation: AIR1997SC2523, 1997(99(2))BOMLR416, (1997)141CTR(SC)67, [1997]226ITR625(SC), JT1997(5)SC529, 1997(4)SCALE271, (1997)5SCC482, [1997]Supp1SCR394, [1997]92TAXMAN541(SC), MANU/SC/0649/1997

Case Note:

Direct Taxation - Income from House Property - Section 22 of Income Tax Act, 1961 - Tribunal and Appellate authority held that income from flats should be assessed as income from house property under Section 22 and not as income from other sources under Section 56 of Act - High Court reversed finding of Tribunal - Hence, this Appeal - Whether, income derived by Assessee from flats was taxable under head income from other sources and not income from house property - Held, in common law owner mean a person who had got valid title legally conveyed to him after complying with requirements of law such as Transfer of Property Act, Registration Act, etc - However, in context of Section 22 of IT Act having regard to ground realities and further having regard to object of IT Act, owner was a person who was entitled to receive income from property in his own right - Therefore, Tribunal was not justified in holding that income derived by Assessee from flats was taxable under head income from other sources - Thus, Civil Appeal No. 4165/94 dismissed and Civil Appeal No. 4549/ allowed.

Ratio Decidendi:

"There is no presumption as to a tax."

No. of pages in the original judgement: 13

Brief facts of the case:

The respondent in Tax Reference Case Nos. 9-10/86 is a company and an assessee under the Act (hereinafter called the 'assessee'). It owns four flats bearing Nos. 231, 232, 241 and 242 in a building call as "Silver Arch" on Nepeansea Road, Bombay. The builders of the said building are M/s. Malabar Industries Pvt. Ltd. Out of the four aforesaid flats, two were directly purchased by the respondent-company from the builders and the other two were purchased by its sister concern and subsequently by the assessee. The possession of the flats was taken after payment of consideration in full some time in August, 1973. It is common ground that all these flats have been let out to various persons. The rental income from these flats was included in the Return for the assessment years in question, namely, 1975-76 and 1976-77. It was the case of the assessee that the rental income from the flats was assessable as 'income from other sources' under Section 56 of the Act inasmuch as the assessee-company was not the 'legal owner' of the property in the flats. Such a claim was put forward before the Assessing Officer mainly on the ground that the title to the property (four flats) had not been conveyed to the Co-operative society which was formed by the purchasers of the flats and that so long as the ownership was not transferred in the name of the assessee the rental income from the flats could not be assessed as 'income from house property' (under Section 22 of the Act).

One other subsidiary question was also raised by the assessee that the rental income should be calculated on the bonafide annual value and not the actual rent received. As a matter of fact, the assessee has shown Rs. 49,800 as chargeable rent. The Income Tax Officer, however, has taken the annual letting value of those flats at Rs. 1,31,268 on the basis of rent receivable in respect of flats from an adjoining building. The Income Tax

Officer also rejected the claim of the assessee that the income from the flats should be assessed under Section 56 of the Act.

Held,

From the circumstances narrated above and from the Memorandum explaining the Finance Bill, 1987 (supra), it is crystal clear that the amendment was intended to supply an obvious omission or to clear up doubts as to the meaning of the word "owner" in Section 22 of the Act. We do not think that in the light of the clear exposition of the position of a declaratory/clarificatory Act it is necessary to multiply the authorities on this point. We have, therefore, no hesitation to hold that the amendment introduced by the Finance Bill, 1988 was declaratory/clarificatory in nature so far as it relates to Section 27(iii), (iiia) and (iiib). Consequently, these provisions are retrospective in operation. If so, the view taken by the High Courts of Patna, Rajasthan, and Calcutta, as noticed above, gets added support and consequently the contrary view taken by the Delhi, Bombay and Andhra Pradesh High Courts is not good law.

We are conscious of the settled position that under the common law owner means a person who has not valid title legally conveyed to him after complying with the requirements of law such as Transfer of Property Act, Registration Act etc. But in the context of Section 22 of the Income-tax Act having regard to the ground realities and further having regard to the object of the Income-tax Act, namely, 'to tax the income', we are of the view, owner' is a person who is entitled to receive income from the property in his own right.

In the light of the above narration and discussion, we do not think it necessary to discuss any more separately the submissions advanced across the bar.

In-time, we answer the question referred to this court in T.R.C. Nos. 9-10/88 in the negative and in favour of the Revenue. The Civil Appeal No. 4165/94 filed by the Revenue stands dismissed and Civil Appeal No. 4549/95 by an assessee stands allowed. However, there will be no order as to costs.

ÞÞÞ

ELEVEN

Malayala Manorama Co. Ltd. Vs. Commissioner of Income Tax, Trivandrum, 2008

Hon'ble Judges/Coram: Ashok Bhan and Dalveer Bhandari, JJ.

Relevant Section:

INCOME-TAX ACT, 1961 - Section 115J

Equivalent Citation: (2010)5CompLJ12(SC), (2008)216CTR(SC)102, [2008]300ITR251(SC), JT2008(5)SC529, 2008(6)SCALE659, (2008)12SCC612, [2008]169TAXMAN471(SC), MANU/SC/7558/2008

No. of pages in the original judgement: 10

Case Note:

Direct Taxation - Income Tax - Jurisdiction of Income Tax Officer to rework net profits - Section 115J of Income Tax Act, 1961 - Whether in respect of a company consistently charging depreciation in its books of account at the rates prescribed in the Income-tax Rules, the Income Tax Officer has jurisdiction under Section 115J of the Income Tax Act, 1961 to rework net profits by substituting the rates prescribed in Schedule XIV of the Companies Act, 1956 - Held, it was held in Apollo Tyres Ltd. etc. v. Commissioner of Income Tax, Kochi etc that the Assessing Officer while computing the income under Section 115J has only the power of examining whether the books of account are certified by the authorities under the Companies Act as having been properly maintained in accordance with the Companies Act i.e. the Assessing Officer does not have the jurisdiction to go behind the net profit shown in the profit and loss account except to the extent provided in the Explanation to Section 115J - Appeal allowed

Ratio Decidendi:

The Assessing Officer does not have the jurisdiction to go behind the net profit shown in the profit and loss account except to the extent provided in the Explanation to Section 115J

Brief facts of the case:

These appeals are directed against the judgment passed by a Division Bench of the Kerala High Court at Ernakulam on 13th November, 2001 whereby the High Court has decided Income Tax Reference Nos.245, 259, 289 and 293 of 1999 by a common judgment.

The main question which arose for consideration before the Court below was:

Whether in respect of a company consistently charging depreciation in its books of account at the rates prescribed in the Income-tax Rules, the Income Tax Officer has jurisdiction under Section 115J of the Income Tax Act, 1961 to rework net profits by substituting the rates prescribed in Schedule XIV of the Companies Act, 1956?

Held,

Mr. Gulati further submitted that before the High Court, it was argued by counsel for the revenue that Section 205 of the Companies Act, 1956 has been legislatively incorporated into the Income Tax Act for the purposes of Section 115J and since this is a legislation by incorporation, the said provision of the Companies Act, 1956 has to be applied as indicated by that provision in the Companies Act. It was also pointed out that in Section 205 of the Companies Act, it has been provided that for the purposes of calculating depreciation under Section 205(1), the same could be provided to the extent specified under Section 350 of the Companies Act. A reference to Section 350 of the Companies Act would show that the amount of depreciation to be deducted shall be the amount, calculated with reference to the written down value of the assets, as shown by the books of the company at the end of the financial year expiring at the commencement of the Act or immediately thereafter and at the end of each subsequent financial year and the rates specified in Schedule XIV to the Companies Act. Therefore, according to the revenue, the calculation of depreciation in terms of the Companies Act and

Schedule XIV thereof becomes a must, while assessing an assessee under Section 115J of the Income Tax Act.

Mr. Gulati further submitted that the question raised in the case of ***Sona Woolen Mills Pvt. Ltd.*** (supra) shows that the assessee was trying to claim depreciation as per Income Tax Rules on the ground that the same was based on the views expressed by the then chairman of the CBDT in a departmental publication. It is clear that the views expressed by the Chairman of the CBDT cannot override the Act and have clearly to be rejected in case they are not consistent with the Act. He submitted that the Kerala High Court in ***Commissioner of Income Tax v. Dynamic Orthopaedics Pvt. Ltd.* MANU/KE/0325/2002** : [2002]257ITR446(Ker) as well as ***Malayala Manorama*** (supra) and the M.P. High Court in the case of ***Commissioner of Income Tax v. Vandana Rolling Mills Ltd.* MANU/MP/0079/1997** : [1998]234ITR693(MP) have all held that for the purposes of Section 115J of the Act, depreciation could not be calculated as per provisions of the Income Tax Rules. Only the Gujarat High Court in the case of ***Deputy Commissioner of Income Tax v. Vardhman Fabrics (P) Ltd.* MANU/GJ/0032/2002** : [2002]254ITR431(Guj) has upheld the view that the circular of the Company Law Board laid down only minimum depreciation for the purposes of distribution of the dividend and the company could decide to give a higher depreciation. Mr. Gulati also contended that the Punjab & Haryana High Court has preferred to follow the minority view and has ignored the majority view taken by two High Courts, namely the Kerala High Court as well as the M.P. High Court.

29. Mr. Gulati also relied upon the case of ***J.K. Industries Ltd. v. Union of India* MANU/IL/5005/2007**. On proper analysis of the said case, we find that this case also does not help the Revenue.

We have heard the learned Counsel for the parties at length and carefully perused the written submissions filed by them. In our considered opinion, the controversy involved in this case is no longer *res integra*. A three Judge Bench of this Court in ***Apollo Tyres*** (supra) has clearly interpreted Section 115J of the 1961 Act. There is no scope for any further discussion.

Consequently, the appeals are allowed and the impugned order of the High Court is accordingly set aside. In the facts and circumstances of the case, we direct the parties to bear their own costs.

PPP

TWELVE

SYNCO INDUSTRIES LTD. VS. ASSESSING OFFICER, INCOME TAX, MUMBAI AND ORS., 2008

Hon'ble Judges/Coram: Ashok Bhan and J.M. Panchal, JJ.

Relevant Section:

INCOME-TAX ACT, 1961 - Section 80I; INCOME-TAX ACT, 1961 - Section 80HH, INCOME-TAX ACT, 1961 - Section 80B(5), INCOME-TAX ACT, 1961 - Section 80AB, INCOME-TAX ACT, 1961 - Section 80A

Equivalent Citation: 1(2008)CLT804, (2008)215CTR(SC)385, [2008]299ITR444(SC), JT2008(4)SC1, 2008(4)SCALE263, (2008)4SCC22, [2008]168TAXMAN224(SC), MANU/SC/7257/2008

No. of pages in the original judgement: 8

Case Note: Direct Taxation - Income Tax - Deduction - Section 80-A of the Income Tax Act, 1948 - Appellant had earned profit in both the units - As the appellant had suffered losses in the oil division in earlier years, claimed deductions under Section 80HH and 80-I, claiming that each unit should be treated separately and the loss suffered by the oil division in earlier years is not adjustable against the profits of the chemical division while considering the question whether deductions under Sections 80HH and 80-I were allowable - Whether the gross total income must be determined by setting off against the income, the business losses of the earlier years, before allowing deduction under Chapter VI-A and if the resultant income is "Nil", then the assessee cannot claim deduction under Chapter VI-A of the Income Tax Act, 1948 - Held, the gross total income of the assessee has first got to be determined after adjusting losses etc., and if the gross total income of the assessee is 'Nil' the assessee would not be entitled to deductions under Chapter VI-A of the Act - Appeals dismissed.

Ratio Decidendi:

Gross total income of the assessee has first got to be determined after adjusting losses etc., and if the gross total income of the assessee is 'Nil' the assessee would not be entitled to deductions under Chapter VI-A.

Brief facts of the case:

The appellant-assessee is a Company incorporated under the provisions of the Indian Companies Act, 1956. It is engaged in the business of oil and chemicals. It has a unit for oil division at Sirohi District, Rajasthan. It has also a chemical division at Jodhpur. The appellant had earned profit in the assessment year 1990-91 and 1991-92 in both the units. However, the appellant had suffered losses in the oil division in earlier years. The appellant claimed deductions under Section 80HH and 80-I of the Act, claiming that each unit should be treated separately and the loss suffered by the oil division in earlier years is not adjustable against the profits of the chemical division while considering the question whether deductions under Sections 80HH and 80-I were allowable. The Assessing Officer noticed that the gross total income of the appellant before deductions under Chapter VI-A was 'Nil'. therefore, he concluded that the assessee was not entitled to the benefit of deductions under Chapter VI-A. Feeling aggrieved the appellant carried the matters in appeal before the Commissioner of Income Tax (Appeals) V, Mumbai who confirmed the view of the Assessing Officer by dismissing the same. therefore, the appellant preferred two appeals before Income Tax Appellate Tribunal Mumbai Bench 'B', Mumbai. The Tribunal held that gross total income of the appellant had got to be computed in accordance with the Act before allowing deductions under any Section falling under Chapter VI-A and as the gross total income of the appellant after setting off the business losses of the earlier years, was 'Nil', the appellant was not entitled to any deductions either under Section 80HH or 80-I of the Act. In that view of the matter the Tribunal dismissed the appeals filed by the appellant. Thereupon, the appellant invoked jurisdiction of the High Court under Section 260-A of the Act by filing these appeals. The High

Court has dismissed the same by Judgment dated July 23, 2001 giving rise to the instant appeals.

This Court has heard the learned Counsel for the parties at length and in great detail. This Court has also considered the documents forming part of the appeals.

Held,

The contention that under Section 80-I (6) the profits derived from one industrial undertaking cannot be set off against loss suffered from another and the profit is required to be computed as if profit making industrial undertaking was the only source of income, has no merits. Section 80-I (1) lays down that where the gross total income of the assessee includes any profits derived from the priority undertaking/unit/division, then in computing the total income of the assessee, a deduction from such profits of an amount equal to 20% has to be made. Section 80-I (1) lays down the broad parameters indicating circumstances under which an assessee would be entitled to claim deduction. On the other hand Section 80-I (6) deals with determination of the quantum of deduction. Section 80-I (6) lays down the manner in which the quantum of deduction has to be worked out. After such computation of the quantum of deduction, one has to go back to Section 80-I (1) which categorically states that where the gross total income includes any profits and gains derived from an industrial undertaking to which Section 80-I applies then there shall be a deduction from such profits and gains of an amount equal to 20%. The words "includes any profits" used by the legislature in Section 80-I(1) are very important which indicate that the gross total income of an assessee shall include profits from a priority undertaking. While computing the quantum of deduction under Section 80-I(6) the Assessing Officer, no doubt, has to treat the profits derived from an industrial undertaking as the only source of income in order to arrive at the deduction under Chapter VI-A. However, this Court finds that the non-obstante clause appearing in Section 80-I(6) of the Act, is applicable only to the quantum of deduction, whereas, the gross total income under Section 80B(5) which is also referred to in Section 80I(1) is required to be computed in the manner provided under the Act which presupposes that the gross total income shall be arrived at after adjusting the losses of the other division against the profits derived from an industrial undertaking. If the interpretation as suggested by the appellant is accepted it would almost render the provisions of Section 80A(2) of the Act nugatory and therefore the interpretation canvassed on behalf of the appellant cannot be accepted.

It is true that under Section 80-I(6) for the purpose of calculating the deduction, the loss sustained in one of the units, cannot be taken into account because Sub-section 6 contemplates that only the profits shall be taken into account as if it was the only source of income. However, Section 80A(2) and Section 80B (5) are declaratory in nature. They apply to all the Sections falling in Chapter VI-A. They impose a ceiling on the total amount of deduction and therefore the non-obstante clause in Section 80-I(6) cannot restrict the operation of Sections 80A(2) and 80B(5) which operate in different spheres. As observed earlier Section 80-I(6) deals with actual computation of deduction whereas Section 80- I(1) deals with the treatment to be given to such deductions in order to arrive at the total income of the assessee and therefore while interpreting Section 80-I(1), which also refers to gross total income one has to read the expression 'gross total income' as defined in Section 80B(5). therefore, this Court is of the opinion that the High Court was justified in holding that the loss from the oil division was required to be adjusted before determining the gross total income and as the gross total income was 'Nil' the assessee was not entitled to claim deduction under Chapter VI-A which includes Section 80-I also.

The proposition of law, emerging from the above discussion is that the gross total income of the assessee has first got to be determined after adjusting losses etc., and if the gross total income of the assessee is 'Nil' the assessee would not be entitled to deductions under Chapter VI-A of the Act.

The appeals therefore filed by the appellant have no substance and deserve to be dismissed. Accordingly, all the appeals fail and are dismissed. There shall be no order as to cost.

THIRTEEN

COMMNR. OF INCOME TAX-I, AHMEDABAD VS. GOLD COIN HEALTH FOOD PVT. LTD., 2008

Hon'ble Judges/Coram: Dr. Arijit Pasayat, P. Sathasivam and Aftab Alam, JJ.

Relevant Section:

INCOME-TAX ACT, 1961 - Section 27(1)C

Equivalent Citation: 2008(70)AIC206, (2008)218CTR(SC)359, [2008]304ITR308(SC), JT2008(9)SC312, 2008(11)SCALE492, (2008)9SCC622, [2008]172TAXMAN386(SC), 2008(2)UJ1144, MANU/SC/3523/2008

No. of pages in the original judgement: 8

Case Note:

Direct Taxation - Penalty - Levy of - Section 271(1)(c) of the Income TaxAct, 1961 - Amendment made by Finance Act, 2002 w.e.f. 1st April, 2003in Explanation 4 to Section 271(1)(c)(iii) - Period of dispute being 1st April, 1976to 1st April, 2003 - Reference made expressing doubt about the correctness of the Judgment of Virtual Soft Systems Ltd. v. Commissioner of Income Tax, Delhi- Whether amendment made to the Section 271(1)(c)(iii) by the Finance Act, 2002 was clarificatory in nature and consequentially it was applicable retrospectively - Whether the penalty under Section 271(1)(c)can be levied if the returned income, not declared, is a loss – Appellant contended that the purpose behind Section 271(1)(c) is to penalize the Assessee for (a) concealing particulars of the income; and/or (b) furnishing inaccurate particulars of such income and whether income returned was a profit or loss was really of no consequence - Per contra Respondent contended that amendment and the Explanation 4(a) carried out, enlarged the scope for levying penalty under Section 271(1)(c) and, therefore, does not operate retrospectively and is applicable only w.e.f. 1st April, 2003 - Held, expression "income" should be understood to include losses - Finance Act intention was to make the position explicit which otherwise was implied - Explanation 4(a) to Section 271(1)(c) intended to levy the penalty not only in a case where after addition of concealed income, a loss returned, after assessment becomes positive income but also in a case where addition of concealed income reduces the returned loss and finally the assessed income is also a loss or a minus figure- therefore, even during the period between 1st April, 1976 to 1st April, 2003the position was that the penalty was leviable even in a case where addition of concealed income reduces the returned loss - It may also include carried forward loss which is required to be set up against future income under Section 72 of the Act - Hence, the applicable law on the date of filing of the return cannot be confined only to the losses of the previous accounting years- Explanation 4 to Section 271(1)(c) is clarificatory and not substantive -Views expressed in Virtual Soft contrary - Appeals disposed of

Ratio Decidendi:

"Explanation 4(a) to Section 271(1)(c) of Income tax Act intended to levy the penalty not only in a case where after addition of concealed income, a loss returned after assessment becomes positive income but also in a case where addition of concealed income reduces the returned loss and finally the assessed income is also a loss or a minus figure."

Brief facts of the case:

Expressing doubt about the correctness of the judgment rendered by a Division Bench of this Court in Virtual Soft Systems Ltd. v. Commissioner of Income Tax, Delhi MANU/SC/0879/2007 : : [2007]289ITR83(SC), a reference has been made by another Division Bench by order dated 7.4.2008 to a larger Bench. The question which was decided in Virtual's case (supra) was as to whether the penalty under Section 271(1)(c) of the Income Tax Act, 1961 (in short the `Act') can be levied if the returned income is a loss. This question has to be considered in the background of the amendment made by Finance Act, 2002 (in short `Finance Act') w.e.f. 1.4.2003 in Explanation 4 to Section 271(1)(c)(iii) of the Act. In Virtual's case (supra) the department placed reliance on Notes on Clauses relating to the aforesaid amendment to submit that the amendment was clarificatory in nature and consequentially it was applicable retrospectively. This argument was rejected by this Court in para 52 of the judgment. The Division Bench while making reference was of the view that the true effect of the amendment was not considered, as it was prima facie of the view that merely because the amendment was stated to take effect from 1.4.2003 that cannot be a ground to hold that the same did have the retrospective effect.

Learned Counsel for the appellant submitted that the true scope and ambit of the amendment has been lost sight of in Virtual Soft's case (supra). It is submitted that the purpose behind Section 271(1)(c) is to penalize the assessee for (a) concealing particulars of the income; and/or (b) furnishing inaccurate particulars of such income. therefore, whether income returned was a profit or loss was really of no consequence.

Held,

Above being the position, the inevitable conclusion is that Explanation 4 to Section 271(1)(c) is clarificatory and not substantive. The view expressed to the contrary in Virtual's case (supra) is not correct.

So far as the appeal relating to SLP (C) No. 4379 of 2007 is concerned, it is to be noted that learned Solicitor General has stated that even if the Department succeeds ultimately before this Bench, they would not demand penalty from the assessee in that case. Similar is the position in civil Appeal relating to SLP(C) No. 14785 of 2007.

The appeals are disposed of.

FOURTEEN

Commissioner of Income Tax, Ahmedabad Vs. Sarabhai Holdings Pvt. Ltd., 2008

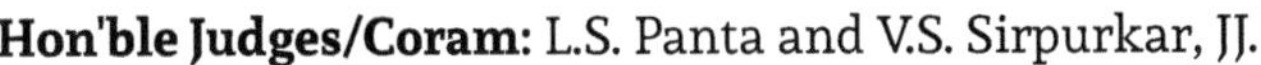

Hon'ble Judges/Coram: L.S. Panta and V.S. Sirpurkar, JJ.

Relevant Section:

INCOME-TAX ACT, 1961 - Section 273(2)(A)

Equivalent Citation: (2008)219CTR(SC)644, [2008]307ITR89(SC), JT2008(12)SC464, 2008(14)SCALE454, (2009)1SCC28, [2008]175TAXMAN82(SC), MANU/SC/8137/2008

No. of pages in the original judgement: 10

Case Note:

Direct Taxation - Interest accrued - Advance Tax - Mens rea - Section 273(2)(a) of the Income Tax Act, 1961 - Assessee filed return for the assessment year 1979-80 declaring total income of Rs. 772 - For Assessment year 1980-81 Assessee filed return declaring loss of Rs. 17,345 - Assessing Officer passed assessment Order determining total income which included interest accrued on deferred sale consideration received from sale of subsidiary - Interest also levied as Assessee failed to pay advance tax and directed initiation of penalty proceedings against Assessee - In appeals filed by Assessee before Commissioner of Income Tax (Appeals) assessment Order was upheld and waiver of interest by Resolution dated 30th June, 1978 was rejected - High Court did away with penalty - Held, No ill intention on part of Assessee to evade tax - Said interest cannot be treated as income so as to compel Assessee to pay advance tax - No justification for a show cause notice under Section 274 read with Section 273(2)(a) of the Act on the ground that the Assessee had deliberately filed an untrue estimate of the advance tax which he had known or reason to believe to be untrue - Appeals dismissed.

Brief facts of the case:

This Judgment will dispose of two Appeals, they being civil Appeal Nos. 482 of 2003 and 483 of 2003. These Appeals are filed by the Commissioner of Income Tax, Ahmedabad (hereinafter referred to as "Revenue"). In both the Appeals, the Revenue challenges the common judgment passed by the Gujarat High Court, wherein, the High Court was considering Income Tax Reference (ITR) Nos. 56 of 1986, 58 of 1993, 220 of 1995 and 75 of 1987. These References were made out of the order of Income Tax Appellate Tribunal (hereinafter referred to as "the Tribunal").

It is agreed before us that presently we would be concerned only with two References, they being Reference No. 56 of 1986 and Reference No. 220 of 1995. Insofar as Reference No. 75 of 1987 is concerned, though the High Court had answered in favour of Revenue and against the assessee, the assessee did not file any appeal and, therefore, that part of the High Court Judgment dealing with Income Tax Reference No. 75 of 1987 becomes final. The learned Counsel for the assessee very fairly agreed with the same. As regards the Income Tax Reference No. 58 of 1993, the Revenue had filed an appeal against the impugned judgment dealing with the same, however, this Court had dismissed the appeal filed by the Revenue on the grounds of limitation. The learned Senior Counsel Mr. P.V. Shetty, appearing on behalf of the Revenue very fairly admitted this position. We are, therefore, left with only two References, which are as under:

Income Tax Reference No. 56 of 1986

(which emanated from the quantum proceedings in respect of the Assessment Years 1979-80 and 1980-81):

Held,

The specific wording would signify that there has to be a satisfaction of the Assessing Officer that the estimate of advance tax furnished by the assessee was not only untrue, but the assessee also knew or had reason to believe the same to be untrue. In the present case, there can be no dispute that the claim of the assessee in respect of the Assessment Year 1979-80 was not accepted. However, in our opinion, in the peculiar facts of this case, it cannot be said that the assessee had knowledge of its estimate of advance tax to be untrue or had reason to believe the same to be untrue. The assessee had, undoubtedly, claimed the waiving of that interest as a natural corollary of the Resolution dt. 30.6.1978. It was also claimed that the assessee had commercial expediency for doing the same. It was tried to show that such commercial expediency arose by the subsequent agreement, whereby, the Elscope had agreed to provide the security for the amount due from it. Assessee had, therefore, furnished its estimate for the advance tax as Nil, as it claimed that it had the income of only about Rs. 800/-. In the subsequent year, the assessee claimed the loss of about Rs. 17,000/-. Though the attempt on the part of the assessee was to give up the accrued interest in the name of commercial expediency, there was no valid justification to relinquish the same, as has been found by the High Court. The High Court has also specifically found that the only aim was to avoid payment of tax which had become due on the basis of the accrual of interest and commercial expediency was only a dignified guard in which the arrangement made to evade the tax was sought to be covered. However, it was shown to the High Court that the penalties levied under Section 273(2)(a) of the Act were determined in case of two companies of the same Group, they being, Fabriquip Pvt. Ltd. and Packart Pvt. Ltd., wherein, it was held that the Resolution passed on 30.06.1978 for the foregoing interest had become applicable from 1.7.1978. The High Court took the view that the levy of interest under Section 215 of the Act and the levy of penalty under Section 273(2)(a) of the Act stand on different footings. We have no hesitation to accept this view of the High Court. Indeed, while the levy of interest under Section 215 of the Act is automatic, that is not the case with the penalty under Section 273(2)(a) of the Act, where the mens rea on the part of the assessee would have to be shown to the extent, it has been indicated in the language of the Section, where, therefore, there was some scope for the assessee to justify the estimate given by it and that the penalty could not be inflicted. Indeed, if the assessee in this case proceeded on the basis of Resolution dt. 30.6.1978, it has to be held that the assessee had reasonably believed that the income of interest which was written off by the Resolution, could not be added to its income. If it genuinely proceeded under that bonafide impression, then in our opinion, the High Court was right in writing off the penalty and upsetting the view of the Tribunal. We accept the finding of the High Court, which is in the following words:

...no definite conclusion can be drawn that the Assessee had reason to believe that the Nil estimate filed by it was untrue....

Considering the overall facts in this case, we are of the clear opinion that the High Court was right in setting aside the penalty of Rs. 4 lakhs inflicted against the assessee under Section 273(2)(a) of the Act. We answer the issue accordingly. In the result, the appeals filed by the Revenue fail and the judgment of the High Court is confirmed without any costs.

ÞÞÞ

FIFTEEN

Assistant Commissioner, Income Tax, Rajkot Vs. Saurashtra Kutch Stock Exchange Ltd., 2008

Hon'ble Judges/Coram: C.K. Thakker and L.S. Panta, JJ.

Relevant Section:

INCOME-TAX ACT, 1961 - Section 254(2), INCOME-TAX ACT, 1961 - Section 012A, INCOME-TAX ACT, 1961 - Section 11

Equivalent Citation: (2008)219CTR(SC)90, 2008(230)ELT385(S.C.), [2008]305ITR227(SC), JT2008(10)SC306, 2008(12)SCALE582, (2008)14SCC171, 2010[18]S.T.R.84(S.C.), [2008]173TAXMAN322(SC), (2009)11Vat Reporter 19, MANU/SC/4034/2008

No. of pages in the original judgement: 10

Case Note:

Direct Taxation - Mistake apparent from the record - Ground for setting aside an Order - Power of Appellate Tribunal - Sub-section (2) of Section 254of the Income Tax Act, 1961 - Section 11 of Income Tax Act - Assessee filed Miscellaneous Application under Sub-section (2) of Section 254 of the Act in the Tribunal for rectifying an error committed by Tribunal in the decision rendered by it in appeal and also for recalling the Order – Tribunal allowed the application and held that there was a 'mistake apparent from the record' as there was non-consideration of a decision of Jurisdictional Court- Accordingly, it recalled its earlier order - Whether the Income Tax Appellate Tribunal, was right in exercising power under Sub-section (2) of Section 254 of the Act on the ground that there was a 'mistake apparent from the record' committed by the Tribunal while deciding the appeal and whether it could have recalled the earlier order on that ground – Whether non-consideration of a decision of Jurisdictional Court or of the Supreme Court can be said to be a 'mistake apparent from the record' - Held, if Tribunal has exercised power of review, the Order passed by the Tribunal must be set aside - If Tribunal has merely rectified a mistake apparent from the record, it was within the power of the Tribunal and no grievance can be made against exercise of such power - A patent, manifest and self-evident error which does not require elaborate discussion of evidence or argument to establish it, can be said to be an error apparent on the face of the record and can be corrected while exercising certiorari jurisdiction -An error cannot be said to be apparent on the face of the record if one has to travel beyond the record to see whether the Judgment is correct or not -Judicial decision acts retrospectively - Ratio of judgment in Hiralal Bhagwativ. Commissioner of Income Tax was decided few months prior to impugned decision, but it was not brought to the attention of the Tribunal - Hence, such a mistake can be said to be a "mistake apparent from the record" which could be rectified under Section 254(2) - Tribunal has not committed any error of law or of jurisdiction in exercising power under Sub-section (2)of Section 254 of the Act and in rectifying "mistake apparent from the record"- High Court also not wrong in confirming the same - No interference called for - Appeal dismissed

Ratio Decidendi:

"If the Tribunal has merely rectified a mistake apparent from the record the nit was within the power of the Tribunal and no grievance can be made against exercise of such power."

Brief facts of the case:

The present appeal is directed against the judgment and order passed by the High Court of Gujarat, Ahmedabad on March 31, 2003 in Special Civil Application No. 1247 of 2002 [*Assistant Commissioner of Income-Tax v. Saurashtra Kutch Stock Exchange Ltd.* MANU/GJ/0034/2003 : [2003]262ITR146(Guj)]. By the said judgment, the High Court confirmed the order passed by the Income Tax Appellate Tribunal, Ahmedabad on September 5, 2001 in Misc. Application NO. 31/Rjt/2000. By the said order, the Tribunal held that there was a `mistake apparent from the record' within the meaning of Sub-section (2) of Section 254 of the Income Tax Act, 1961 and accordingly, it recalled its earlier order passed on October 27, 2000 in ITA No. 69/Rjt/2000.

Shortly stated the facts of the case are that Saurashtra Kutch Stock Exchange Ltd.- respondent herein is an assessee under the Income Tax Act, 1961 (hereinafter referred to as `the Act'). It is a Company registered under Section 25 of the Companies Act, 1956. The assessee is a `Stock Exchange' duly recognized under the Securities Contracts (Regulation) Act, 1956. As a `Stock Exchange', it is a `charitable institution' entitled to exemption under Sections 11 and 12 of the Act from payment of income-tax. The assessee, therefore, made an application on February 10, 1992 for registration under Section 12A of the Act. The Commissioner of Income Tax, Rajkot registered it on July 8, 1996. The assessee filed its return of income on October 29, 1996 for the assessment year 1996-97 declaring its total taxable income as `Nil', claiming exemption under Section 11 of the Act although the assessee had not been registered under Section 12A of the Act. The return was processed under Sub-section (1)(a) of Section 143 of the Act. On November 7, 1997, a notice was issued to the assessee by the Commissioner of Income Tax under Section 154 of the Act to show cause why exemption granted under Section 11 of the Act should not be withdrawn. The assessee replied to the said notice and asserted that in accordance with Section 12A of the Act, the trust had made an application for registration and, hence, it was entitled to exemption under Section 11 of the Act. Meanwhile, the Commissioner of Income Tax on February 20, 1998 granted registration to the assessee on condition that the eligibility regarding exemption under Section 11 of the Act would be examined by the Assessing Officer for each assessment year.

Held,

In the present case, according to the assessee, the Tribunal decided the matter on October 27, 2000. Hiralal Bhagwati was decided few months prior to that decision, but it was not brought to the attention of the Tribunal. In our opinion, in the circumstances, the Tribunal has not committed any error of law or of jurisdiction in exercising power under Sub-section (2) of Section 254 of the Act and in rectifying "mistake apparent from the record". Since no error was committed by the Tribunal in rectifying the mistake, the High Court was not wrong in confirming the said order. Both the orders, therefore, in our opinion, are strictly in consonance with law and no interference is called for.

For the foregoing reasons, in our view, no case has been made out to interfere with the order passed by the Income Tax Appellate Tribunal, Ahmedabad and confirmed by the High Court of Gujarat. The appeal deserves to be dismissed and is accordingly dismissed. On the facts and in the circumstances of the case, however, the parties are ordered to bear their own costs.

Before parting, we may state that we have not stated anything on the merits of the matter. As indicated earlier, the assessee has not approached this Court. Only the Revenue has challenged the order passed under Section 254(2) of the Act. The Tribunal, in view of the order of rectification, has directed the Registry to fix the matter for re-hearing and as such the appeal will be heard on merits. We, therefore, clarify that we may not be understood to have expressed any opinion one way or the other so far as exemption from payment of tax claimed by the assessee is concerned. As and when the Tribunal will hear the matter, it will decide on its own merit without being influenced by any observations made by it in the impugned order or in the order of the High Court or in this judgment.

Ordered accordingly.

SIXTEEN

Deputy Commissioner of Income Tax, Ahmedabad Vs. Core Health Care Ltd., 2008

Hon'ble Judges/Coram: S.H. Kapadia and B. Sudershan Reddy, JJ.

Relevant Section:

INCOME-TAX ACT, 1961 - Section 260A, INCOME-TAX ACT, 1961 - Section 080I, INCOME-TAX ACT, 1961 - Section 080HH, INCOME-TAX ACT, 1961 - Section 37, INCOME-TAX ACT, 1961 - Section 36(1)(iii), INCOME-TAX ACT, 1961 - Section 035D, INCOME-TAX ACT, 1961 - Section 32

Equivalent Citation: 105(2008)CLT433(SC), (2008)215CTR(SC)1, [2008]298ITR194(SC), JT2008(2)SC367, 2008(2)SCALE327, (2008)2SCC465, MANU/SC/0962/2008

No. of pages in the original judgement: 6

Case Note:

Direct Taxation - Capital assets - Borrowings - Interest paid - Deduction - Section 36(1)(iii) of Income Tax Act, 1961 - Assessee claimed deduction towards expenses aggregating which included interest on borrowings - During assessment year under consideration Assessee had installed new machinery - Assessing Officer disallowed the deductions - On appeal CIT (A) confirmed the addition of interest amount on borrowings to the income of the Assessee - However, Tribunal and thereafter High Court held that the Assessing Officer was not justified in making disallowance in respect of borrowings utilized for purchase of machinery - Hence, the present appeal - Whether interest paid in respect of borrowings on capital assets not put to use in the concerned financial year can be permitted as allowable deduction under Section 36(1)(iii) - Held, Section 36(1)(iii) is attracted when the Assessee borrows the capital for the purpose of his business - It does not matter whether the capital is borrowed in order to acquire a Revenue asset or a capital asset, because Section requires is that the Assessee must borrow the capital for the purpose of his business - In the present case, even though the machinery has not been actually used in the business at the time when the assessment was made, the same has to be treated as a business asset as it was purchased only for business purposes - In the circumstances, the interest paid on the amount borrowed for purpose of such machinery is certainly a deductible amount - Assessing Officer not justified in making disallowance in respect of borrowings utilised for purchase of machines - Question answered in favour of the assessee and against the Department

Brief facts of the case:

These civil appeals are directed against judgment and order dated 25.4.01 delivered by Gujarat High Court in Tax Appeal Nos. 449 and 450 of 2000 and in Civil Application Nos. 53 and 54 of 2001 whereby the Department's appeals, under Section 260A of the Income-tax Act, 1961, stood dismissed.

On 31.12.92 assessee filed its return of income for A.Y. 1992-93 declaring "nil" income. Later on the assessee filed a revised return on 6.8.93 declaring a loss of Rs. 1,11,68,543/-. Assessee-company is engaged in the business of manufacturing and sale of intravenous solutions. For the assessment year under consideration assessee claimed deduction towards expenses aggregating to Rs. 2,12,05,459/-which included interest on borrowings of Rs. 1,56,76,000/-. During the assessment year under consideration assessee had installed new machinery. The A.O. vide assessment order dated 30.3.95 disallowed the amount of Rs. 1,56,76,000/-placing reliance on the judgment of this Court in **Challapalli Sugars Ltd. and Anr.** v. **Commissioner of Income-tax, A.P. and Anr.**MANU/SC/0241/1974 : [1975]98ITR167(SC) , inter alia, on the ground that during the assessment year under consideration assessee had installed new machinery on which production had not started. On appeal, vide order dated 15.11.96, CIT (A) confirmed the addition of interest amount on borrowings of Rs. 1,56,76,000 Therefore, both the authorities, namely, the A.O. and CIT (A) added the said amount of Rs. 1,56,76,000/- to the income of the assessee. The matter was carried in appeal by the assessee. Vide order dated 6.6.2000 the Tribunal held that the Department was not justified in adding Rs. 1,56,76,000/-to the income of the assessee. In other words, the Tribunal held that the A.O. was not justified in making disallowance of Rs. 1,56,76,000/- in respect of borrowings utilized for purchase of machinery. This decision was confirmed by the High Court, hence these civil appeals are filed by the Department.

The following question of law has been placed before us for determination:

Whether interest paid in respect of borrowings on capital assets not put to use in the concerned financial year can be permitted as allowable deduction under Section 36(1)(iii) of the Income-tax Act, 1961?

Held,

Although the Department had moved the said Civil Application Nos. 53 and 54 of 2001 during the pendency of Tax Appeal Nos. 449 and 450 of 2000 well within limitation the High Court without answering the above three questions summarily rejected Civil Application Nos. 53 and 54 of 2001. We are of the view that the High Court had erred in dismissing the above two civil applications for amendment of the Memo of Appeal in Tax Appeal Nos. 449 and 450 of 2000. In our view the above three questions are substantial questions of law and, therefore, the High Court ought to have decided those questions.

Accordingly, we remit the above three questions to the High Court for fresh consideration by it in accordance with law. Accordingly, Civil Appeal Nos. 3952-55 of 2002 and Civil Appeal Nos. 8509-8510 of 2002 filed by the Department are partly allowed with no order as to costs.

SEVENTEEN

IPCA LABORATORY LTD. VS. DEPUTY COMMISSIONER OF INCOME TAX, MUMBAI, 2004

Hon'ble Judges/Coram: S.N. Variava and H.K. Sema, JJ.

Relevant Section:

INCOME-TAX ACT, 1961 - Section 080HHC(4A), INCOME-TAX ACT, 1961 - Section 080HHC(1A), INCOME-TAX ACT, 1961 - Section 080HHC, INCOME-TAX ACT, 1961 - Section 080B(5), INCOME-TAX ACT, 1961 - Section 080AB

Equivalent Citation: 2004(17)AIC862, 2004(106(2))BOMLR406, (2004)187CTR(SC)513, [2004]266ITR521(SC), JT2004(3)SC295, 2004(3)SCALE214, (2004)12SCC742, [2004]2SCR1075, [2004]135TAXMAN594(SC), MANU/SC/0219/2004

No. of pages in the original judgement: 17

Case Note:

Direct Taxation - Income Tax Act - Sections 80AB, 80HHC - Benefit of deduction under Section 80HHC - Entitlement to - Appellants, export house exporting goods self manufactured and trading goods - Claimed deduction under Section 80 HHC for Rs 3.78 crores - Assessing officer holding that Rs 3.78 crores being profit from exports of self manufactured goods and there being loss of Rs 6, 86 crores from exports of trading goods, disallowed deduction of 3.78 crores - Appeal - Dismissed by Commissioner (Appeals) - Second appeal - Dismissed - Appeal to Supreme Court - Dismissing appeal held that if wordings of Section are clear then benefits, which are not available under Section, cannot be conferred by ignoring or misinterpreting words in Section - The opening words "profit derived from such exports" together with word "and" clearly indicate that profits have to be calculated by counting both exports - In arriving at profits earned from export of both self manufactured goods and trading goods, profits and losses in both trades have to be taken into consideration - If after such adjustments there is a positive profit, assessee would be entitled to deduction under Section 80 HHC and if there is a loss he would not be entitled to any deduction

Brief facts of the case:

The Appellants are a Export House. They hold a certificate issued by the Chief Controller of Imports and Exports. For the Assessment Year 1996-97 the Appellants filed a return of income declaring Nil income. It is an admitted position that the taxable income, before the deductions under Chapter VIA, was Ps. 4.39 crores. However, against this taxable income the Appellants claimed various deductions. One such deduction was under Section 80HHC for Rs. 3.78 crores. During the assessment proceedings it was found that the Appellants were exporting goods which were self manufactured as well as goods manufactured by supporting manufacturers i.e. trading goods. It was found that the sum of Rs. 3.78 crores, which had been claimed as a deduction, was the profit from exports of self manufactured goods. It was found that from the exports of trading goods there was a loss of Rs. 6,86 crores. It was found that the Appellants had issued certificates of disclaimer in favour of the supporting manufacturers in respect of the entire export of trading goods. The Assessing Officer therefore held that there was a net loss from export of goods and disallowed the deduction of Rs. 3.78 crores. The Commissioner (Appeals) dismissed the Appeal filed by the Appellants on 11th October, 1999. On 29th December, 2000 the Income Tax Appellate Tribunal dismissed the Second Appeal. By the impugned Judgment the Bombay High Court has dismissed the Appeal filed under Section 260A of the Income Tax Act.

Held,

In our view, the above observations are against the Appellants. They show that in computing income profits and gains, losses must also be taken into consideration.

Mr. Dastur relied on a format of Form No. 10CCAC and a Circular of the Board wherein it is stated as follows:

"With the adoption of the dual system for computing export profit, the computation of the disclaimed export turnover also required modification. The Finance Act has therefore amended Section 80HHCin order to provide that, where the Export or Trading House disclaims the tax concession in favour of the supporting manufacturer, the concession to the Export or Trading House will be reduced by the amount which bears to the total export profits of trading goods the same proportion as the disclaimed export turnover bears to the total export turnover of trading goods. The formula in such cases will now be -

80HHC concession = export profit - [export profits on trading goods x disclaimed export turnover]total export turnover"

Mr. Dastur submitted that if even both profits and losses are to be taken into account the, on a disclaimer the losses will also have to be considered as negative profits and as per the Board Circular the calculation would be as follows:

"80HHC Concession =

```
*Export Profits - [Export Profits on Trading Goods x
 Disclaimed Export Turnover]
 Total Export Turnover of Trading Goods
 = *(-3,07,84,867) - (-6,86,65,804) x  18,53,53,371
                                       18,53,53,371
 = (-3,07,84,867) - (-6,86,65,804)
 = (-3,07,84,867) + 6,85,65,804
 =  3,78,80,937  "
```

He submitted that even on this calculation the Appellants are entitled to deduction of Rs. 3,78,80,937/-. We are unable to accept this submission. The calculation as per the Board Circular would not be as claimed. The Board Circular nowhere provides for negative profits. The Board Circular also shows that only positive profits can be considered for purposes of deduction.

We, therefore, see no substance in the Appeal. The same stands dismissed. There shall be no order as to costs.

EIGHTEEN

Commissioner of Income Tax Vs. P.V.A.L. Kulandagan Chettiar (Dead) through L.Rs., 2004

Hon'ble Judges/Coram: S. Rajendra Babu, C.J. and G.P. Mathur, J.

Relevant Section:

INCOME-TAX ACT, 1961 - Section 90, INCOME-TAX ACT, 1961 - Section 5, INCOME-TAX ACT, 1961 - Section 4

Equivalent Citation: 2004(22)AIC129, [2004]60CLA391(SC), (2004)189CTR(SC)193, [2004]267ITR654(SC), 2004(6)SCALE36, (2004)6SCC235, [2004]Supp(2)SCR697, [2004]137TAXMAN460(SC), MANU/SC/0513/2004

No. of pages in the original judgement: 18

Case Note:

Direct taxation - Income Tax Act, 1961 - Sections 2(24), 4, 5, 6, 10(15), 33, 80J, 80K, 80M, 90, 90(2), 91 and 91(1) - Double taxation - Issue of - Determination of - Agreement between government of India and Government of Malaysia for avoidance of Double Taxation - Respondent firm owning immovable properties at Ipoh, Malaysia - Assessment of incomes of respondent in India - Appeal - Commissioner of Income Tax (Appeals) holding that unless respondent had a permanent establishment of business in India, such business income in Malaysia could not be included in total income of assessee - Appeal - Finding of commissioner upheld by tribunal and High Court - Appeal to Supreme Court - Dismissing appeal held that in case of person being a resident in both contracting states, fiscal domicile with have to be determined with reference to fact that if contracting state with which his personal and economic relations are closer, he would be deemed to be a resident of contracting state in which he had an habitual abode - Immovable property situated in Malaysia and income derived from that property - No permanent establishment in India for carrying on business of rubber plantations in Malaysia out of which income was derived - Business Income out of rubber plantations held not taxable in India due to closer economic relations between assessee and Malaysia in which property was located - Conclusion that capital gains was not income and was not covered by treaty held unsustainable since for purposes of Act, capital gains is always treated as income arising out of immovable property - Findings of High Court held justified.

Brief facts of the case:

These appeals involve following two questions for our consideration although several other questions were considered by the High Court :-

(a) Whether the Malaysian income cannot be subjected to tax in India in the basis of the agreement of avoidance of double taxation entered into between Government of India and Government of Malaysia ?

(b) Whether the capital gains should be taxable only in the country in which the assets are situated?

The facts leading to these appeals are that the respondent is a firm owning immovable properties at Ipoh, Malaysia; that during the course of the assessment year the assessee earned income of Rs. 88,424/- from rubber estates; that the respondent sold property, the short term capital gains of which came to Rs. 18,113/-; that the Income Tax Officer assessed that both the incomes are assessable in India and brought the same to tax; that the respondent filed an appeal before the Commissioner of Income Tax (Appeals) who held that under Article 7(1) of the Avoidance of Double Taxation of Income and Prevention of Fiscal Evasion of Tax unless the respondent has a permanent establishment of the business in India such business income in Malaysia cannot be included in the total income of the assessee and, therefore, no part of the capital gains arising to the respondent in the foreign country could be taxed in India.

Held,

The question as to whether by reason of the sale of the property not having been used whether such income is covered by the Treaty, in the treaty it is specifically provided in Sub-clause (2) of Article II that the agreement shall also apply to any other taxes of a substantially similar character to those referred to in the preceding paragraphs imposed in either contracting State after the date of signature of this agreement. And Income tax is specifically set out in Sub-clause (b) of Clause (1) of Article II. Tax is levied on capital gains and certainly when capital gains is treated as one kind of income tax it also becomes income and assumes substantially similar character of tax referred to in the preceding paragraph.

Taxation policy is within the power of the Government and Section 90 of the Income Tax Act enables the Government to formulate its policy through treaties entered into by it and even such treaty treats the fiscal domicile in one State or the other and thus prevails over the other provisions of the Income Tax Act, it would be unnecessary to refer to the terms addressed in OECD or in any of the decisions of foreign jurisdiction or in any other agreements.

In this view of the matter, it is unnecessary to refer to the decisions cited before us since we have taken the view with reference to clauses see out under the Agreement. We, therefore, find no me it in these appeals and they stand dismissed.

ppp

NINETEEN

K.C. Builders and Ors. Vs. The Assistant Commissioner of Income Tax, 2004

Hon'ble Judges/Coram: B.N. Agrawal and A.R. Lakshmanan, JJ.

Relevant Section:

INCOME-TAX ACT, 1961 - Section 278B, INCOME-TAX ACT, 1961 - Section 277, INCOME-TAX ACT, 1961 - Section 276B, INCOME-TAX ACT, 1961 - Section 271(1)(c), INCOME-TAX ACT, 1961 - Section 254

Equivalent Citation: 2004(16)AIC158, I(2004)CCR207(SC), 2004(1)CTC529, (2004)186CTR(SC)721, [2004]265ITR562(SC), JT2004(2)SC100, 2004(1)KLT596(SC), 2004(2)SCALE137, (2004)2SCC731, [2004]1SCR1134, [2004]135TAXMAN461(SC),MANU/SC/0070/2004

No. of pages in the original judgement: 12

Case Note:

Criminal Procedure Code (CrPC), 1973 - Sections 397 and 401; Income Tax Act, 1961 - Sections 132, 143(3), 147, 148, 254, 256, 256(1), 271, 271(1), 276C(1), 276C(2), 277, 278B and 279(1); Indian Penal Code - Sections 34, 120B, 193, 196 and 420 - Appellant partnership firm engaged in business of construction and Sale of flats, filed returns of income - Since earlier returns found to be defective, appellants filed revised returns - Revised returns accepted by the department - Assessing authority treated difference between income as per original return and revised income as concealed income - Penalties levied under Section 271(1)(c) - Tribunal on appeal held that additions being on basis of settlement between assesses and department, there was no concealment of income - Penalties levied under Section 271(c)(1) cancelled by respondents - Application moved by assessee for dropping criminal proceeding dismissed by magistrate and High Court - Validity - Where an order of assessment or reassessment on basis of which penalty has been levied has itself been finally set aside or cancelled by Tribunal the penalty cannot stand by itself and same is liable to be cancelled - If the Tribunal has set aside the order of concealment and penalties, then there is no concealment in the eyes of law and, prosecution cannot be proceeded with by the complainant and further proceedings would be illegal and without jurisdiction - Since levy, of penalties and prosecution under Section 276C are simultaneous, once penalties are cancelled on ground that there is no concealment, quashing of prosecution under Section 276C is automatic - As under Section 254 of the Act, a finding of Appellate Tribunal supercedes order of Assessing Officer under Section 143(3), entire prosecution becomes devoid of jurisdiction - It being a well-established principle that matter which has been adjudicated and settled by Tribunal need not be dragged into the criminal courts unless and until act of the appellants could have been described as culpable - Since in absence of dishonest and fraudulent intention, question of committing offence under Section 420 of the I.P.C. did not arise, impugned orders passed by High Court set aside.

Brief facts of the case:

These appeals are directed against the final judgment passed by the High Court of Judicature at Madras in Criminal Revision Case No. 508 of 1997 and Criminal Misc. Petition No. 3411 of 1997 dated 13.08.1997 by which the High Court dismissed the criminal revision under Section 397 read with Section 401 of the Code of Criminal Procedure, 1973. The facts giving rise to these appeals are as under-

The appellant is a partnership firm engaged in the business of construction and sale of fiats. The construction of some of the projects started in the year 1981-82 and was completed in the year 1986-87. The appellants filed the returns of income disclosing the assessed income as the income. The cost of construction was shown as under-

Assessment Year 1983-84	-	Rs. 4,72,860/-
Assessment year 1984-85	-	Rs. 77,590/-
Assessment year 1985-86	-	Rs. 7,28,531/-
Assessment year 1986-87	-	Rs. 7,03,002/-

The appellants filed revised returns as per the approved valuer's report for assessment years 1983-84 to 1986-87 on 04.11.1987 in the following manner as the earlier returns were found to be defective with regard to cost of construction.

Assessment year 1983-84	-	Rs. 8,76,000/-
Assessment year 1984-85	-	Rs. 5,42,000/-
Assessment year 1985-86	-	Rs. 13,47,229/-
Assessment year 1986-87	-	Rs. 10,37,920/-

The revised returns were accepted by the Department and assessments were completed.

Held,

In this instant case, the charge of conspiracy has not been proved to bring home the charge of conspiracy within the ambit of Section 120B of I.P.C. It is also settled law that for establishing the offence of cheating the complainant is required to show that the accused had fraudulent or dishonest intention at the time of making promise or misrepresentation. From his making failure to keep up promise subsequently, such a culpable intention right at the beginning that is at the time when the promise was made cannot be presumed. As there was absence of dishonest and fraudulent intention, the question of committing offence under Section 420 of the I.P.C. does not arise.

The High Court without adverting to the above important questions of law involved in this case and examined them in the proper perspective disposed of the revisions in a summary manner and hence the impugned orders passed by the High Court and the learned Magistrate warrant interference.

It is a well-established principle that the matter which has been adjudicated and settled by the Tribunal need not be dragged into the criminal courts unless and until the act of the appellants could have been described as culpable.

For the aforesaid discussions and reasons adduced, the questions of law formulated above are answered accordingly and the appeals stand allowed.

TWENTY

PRAKASH NATH KHANNA AND ORS. VS. COMMISSIONER OF INCOME TAX AND ORS., 2004

Hon'ble Judges/Coram: Doraiswamy Raju and Dr. Arijit Pasayat, JJ.

Relevant Section:

INCOME-TAX ACT, 1961 - Section 278E, INCOME-TAX ACT, 1961 - Section 276CC, INCOME-TAX ACT, 1961 - Section 139

Equivalent Citation: I(2004)CCR276(SC), 2004CriLJ3362, (2004)187CTR(SC)97, [2004]266ITR1(SC), JT2004(2)SC510, 2004(2)SCALE512, (2004)9SCC686, [2004]2SCR434, [2004]135TAXMAN327(SC), MANU/SC/0134/2004

No. of pages in the original judgement: 9

Case Note:

Income Tax Act, 1961 - Sections 139, 139(1), 139(2), 139(3), 139(4), 271(1), 276CC and 278E; Income Tax Act, 1922 - Section 22, 22(1) and 22(3); Taxation Laws (Amendment and Miscellaneous Provisions) Act, 1986 - Section 139(3); Direct Tax Laws (Amendment) Act, 1987 - Section 142(1) - Return of Income of partnership firm was to be filed on or before 31.7.1988 - Return filed by appellants partners of a firm on 20.3.1991 - Initiation of proceedings and imposition of penalty against appellants under Sections 271(1)(a) and 276-CC

- Writ Petition - Dismissed by High Court - Appellants submitted that since return furnished under Section 139(4) at any time before assessment has to be regarded as return furnished under Section 139(1), return was furnished in due time and Section 276-CC was not attracted - Appeal to Supreme Court - Dismissing appeal held that since time within which return is to be furnished is indicated only in sub section (1) of Section 139, even if return is filed in terms of sub section (4) of Section 139, it would not dilute infraction in not furnishing return in due time U/S 139(1) - Infractions covered by Section 276-CC being related to non furnishing of return within time in terms of subsection (1) or (2) of 139, there could not be any condonation of infraction even if return is filed in terms of sub section (4) of 139 - Plea of appellants that provisions of 276-CC would be applicable only in case of there being discovery of failure regarding evasion of tax held unsustainable - Since question whether there was willful failure to furnish the return is a matter to be adjudicated factually by the Court appellant could plead absence of culpable mental state in trial - High Court held justified in dismissing writ petition

Brief facts of the case:

The three appellants were partners of a firm carrying on business under the name and style of M/s Kailash Nath and Associates. Apart from the three appellants, two other persons were partners and one of them Shri Kailash Nath was the Managing partner in terms of the Partnership Deed dated 1.4.1983. For the assessment year 1988-89 return of income was to be filed on or before 31.7.1988, but was in fact filed on 20.3.1991. Assessment under Section 143(3) of the Act was completed on 26.8.1991. Proceedings for late submission of return were initiated against the appellants under Section 271(1)(a) of the Act and penalty was imposed. Proceedings in terms of Section 276CC of the Act were also initiated and complaint was filed before the concerned Court. As noted above, cognizance was taken and process was issued. The writ applications were filed challenging legality of the proceedings. By the impugned judgment the High Court dismissed the writ petitions. The points which were mooted before the High Court were re-iterated in the present appeals.

Mr. G.C. Sharma, learned senior counsel appearing for the appellants urged the following points for consideration:

1. The expression "to furnish in due time" occurring in Section 276CC means to furnish within the time permissible under the Act. The return furnished under Section 139(4) at any time before the assessment is made

has to be regarded as a return furnished under Section 139(1). This was so held by this Court in Commissioner of Income Tax Punjab v. Kullu Valley Transport Co. Pvt. Ltd. MANU/SC/0239/1970 : [1970]77ITR518(SC) in the context of Sections 22(1) and 22(3) of the Indian Income Tax Act, 1922 (in short the 'Old Act') which are in pari-materia of Section 139(1) and Section 139(4) of the Act. It follows that return was furnished in "the due time" and consequently Section 276CC is not attracted.

The provisions of Section 276CC(i) are not intended to apply to the cases of assessees who have been regularly assessed to income tax and have voluntarily submitted their returns of income without issue of any notice to do so by the Assessing Officer in that behalf, within the time permissible to furnish the return under the Act. This interpretation gets support from the marginal heading and explanatory memo laid before Parliament when the Section was introduced.

Held,

Whether there was wilful failure to furnish the return is a matter which is to be adjudicated factually by the Court which deals with the prosecution case. Section 278E is relevant for this purpose and the same reads as follows:

"278-E: Presumption as to culpable mental state-

(1) In any prosecution for any offence under this Act which requires a culpable mental state on the part of the accused, the court shall presume the existence of such mental state but it shall be a defence for the accused to prove the fact that he had no such mental state with respect to the act charged as an offence in that prosecution.

Explanation: In this sub-section, "culpable mental state" includes intention, motive or knowledge of a fact or belief in, or reason to believe, a fact.

(2) For the purposes of this section, a fact is said to be proved only when the court believes it to exist beyond reasonable doubt and not merely when its existence is established by a preponderance of probability:.

There is a statutory presumption prescribed in Section 278E. The Court has to presume the existence of culpable mental state, and absence of such mental state can be pleaded by an accused as a defence in respect to the act charged as an offence in the prosecution. Therefore, the factual aspects highlighted by the appellants were rightly not dealt with by the High Court. This is a matter for trial. It is certainly open to the appellants to plead absence of culpable mental state when the matter is taken up for trial.

Looked at from any angle the appeals are without merit and are dismissed

ÞÞÞ

Videos & Tv Shows On Law & Exim

List of some important videos & TV shows on Law & EXIM by Adv. Jayprakash Somani on his YouTube Channel 'Jayprakash Somani EXIM & Legal'

Legal Videos: Hindi -English

1) SLP in Supreme Court / Special Leave Petitions in the Supreme Court of India

2) Transfer of Civil & Criminal Cases by the Supreme Court of India / Transfer of Matrimonial Cases

3) Appellate Jurisdiction of the Supreme Court of India

4) Jurisdictions of the Supreme Court of India

5) Public Interest Litigation in the Supreme Court of India / PIL in Supreme Court

6) Article 32 Writ Petitions in the Supreme Court of India

7) Bail Matters Top 10 Supreme Court Cases

8) FIR Quashing in High Court & Supreme Court

9) Bail & Anticipatory Bail Matters in Supreme Court

10) Insolvency & Bankruptcy Matters in the Supreme Court

11) Insolvency & Bankruptcy Code 2016 Part 1

12) Insolvency & Bankruptcy Code 2016 Part 2

13) Insolvency & Bankruptcy Code 2016 Part 3

14) Corporate Liquidation Process

15) Supreme Court Rules & Procedures Webinar of 2.5 hour on Zoom

16) RDDBFI Act, 1993 (Introduction)

17) The Indian Contact Act 1872

18) Negotiable Instruments Act (Introduction)

19) How to avoid matrimonial disputes& some more videos

20)SEBI Matters in the Supreme Court

21) Matrimonial Matters: Supreme Court's 20 Case Laws

22) Consumer Matters Supreme Court's 20 Case Laws

23) Service Matters Supreme Court's 20 Case Laws

24) How to Search Lawyer for Your Matter

25) Property Matters Supreme Court's 20 Case Laws

26) Bail Matters: Supreme Court's 20 Case Laws

27) Supreme Court / High Court Vacation Benches

28)69000 Teacher's Recruitment Matters of UP Government in the Supreme Court

29) Contempt of Court Matters in the Supreme Court

30) Advocate Act's Matters in the Supreme Court

31) Business Law Matters in the Supreme Court

32) Banking Matters in the Supreme Court

33) Labour Law Matters in the Supreme Court

34) Arbitration Matters in the Supreme Court

35) Careers in Law -Zoom Webinar by Adv. JayprakashSomani

36) Civil Matters in the Supreme Court

37) Consumer Protection Act | Consumer Matters in the Supreme Court

38) Corporate Matters in the Supreme Court

39) Criminal Matters in the Supreme Court

40) Role of Respondent in the Supreme Court of India

41) Motor Vehicle Accident Matters in Supreme Court with case laws

42) Article 131 Original Suits in Supreme Court

43)PIL in Supreme Court/ Public Interest Litigations in the Supreme Court of India'

44)CAB Citizenship Amendment Bill is not Unconstitutional

45) Supreme Court of India Cases & Process – Marathi

46) Legal Services Export / Export of Legal Services

47) Transfer of Matrimonial Cases by the Supreme Court of India

48) Public Interest Litigation PIL

49) The Specific Relief Act (Introduction)

50) Corporate Insolvency Resolution Process CIRP

51)ABMM's Career 5 - Careers in Law

52) Transfer of cases by Supreme Court

53) Writ Petitions in High Court & Supreme Court of India

54) Supreme Court Jurisdictions - Appeals, SLP, Writ Petitions, Transfer, Original, Review, Curative

55)LEGAL INDIA TV Show: Cases Handled in Supreme Court

56) Corporate Liquidation Process

57) Legal Services Export / Export of Legal Services

EXIM Videos: Hindi -English

1) Yes, I can do Import Export Business Easily! 36 points excellent video in Hindi

2) Yes, I can do Import Export Business Easily! 36 points excellent video in English

3) Import Export Business – Hindi video

4) Import Export Business - English video

5) Export Import Marathi TV Interview

6) Scope for Commerce Students in International Business- TV Show

7) Scope for Management Student in International Business- TV Show

8) Scope for Engineering Students in International Business – TV Show

9) Women in International Business- TV Show

10) How to do Import Export Business Successfully!'

11) Where one can get full information on Import Export Business?

12) What to do import & export?

13) Import Export Workshop/ Training/Course/ Diploma

14) How to Start Import Export Business & How to grow it. Live Webinar

15) Success Stories & Failure Stories in Import & Export Business

16) For MSME Scope in Export & Import...

17) Exports In Agri. & Food Products – English & some more videos

18) Exports to Dubai, Aabudhabii. e. UAE

19) Jewellery Exports from India

20) How to attend EXIM workshop to become excellent Exporter

21) Import Export Best Training Course – Online & Offline

22) Agri Product Export

23) Scope for Woman in International Business

24) Management Graduates Scope in International Business

25) Pharma Product's Export

26) Best Import Export Course | Practical Training | Aaronica Global Exim

27) Import Export Business for Commerce Graduates

28) How Do I Get Export Orders? Finding International Buyers

29) What Is APEDA In Import Export Business?

30) Which Is The Best Product To Export From India?

31)EXIM Remark by Manoj Kumar Faridabad

32)EXIM Remarks by Mahesh Telangana

33) What Licenses I Need To Start Import/ Export?

34) How Can I Increase My Import Export Business?

35) Which Is Best B2B Website For Import/Export Business?

36) Export Import Management with Global Marketing

37) How to Start Export Import Business | 51 Points Video

38) Scope for Commerce & Other Graduates in International Business

39)BE A SUCCESSFUL EXPORTER FOR OUR NATION - Marathi video

40) Export of Textile , Cotton, Agri., Food, & other products & services

41) Exports from MP, CG, MH, GJ & CA in Fresh Fruits & Vegetables

42) Exports in Agri. & Food Products- Hindi

43) Start your Online/E-Commerce Business

44) How to Start Export Import Business & Grow it

45) Exports in Textile & Other Products

46) Start and grow EXIM business - Live English Webinar

47)'Import Export Business!' Why, Who, What & How can one do it easily!!

48) Live: Export of Product & Services During & After Lock Down Period

49) Frauds in Import Export Business

50) Import Export for Business Man

51) Import & Export for Women

51) Import & Export for Graduate & Post - Graduate Students

52) Agriculture Exports from India

53) Digital Marketing Setup - Marathi

54)2nd Secret of Successful Businessman

55) Digital Marketing Set up

56) Legal Services Export / Export of Legal Services

57) Export & Import with UAE

58) Service Exports / Exports by Service Providers

59) Import Export Workshop/ Training/Course/ Diploma

60) Exports & Imports with USA

61) Selection on Product for Export

62) Top Products Exported from India

63) What to do import & export?

64)ABMM Career 2 - 'Careers in Business & Industries

65) How to do Import Export Business Successfully!'

66)5 Secrets of Successful Businessman

67) Export from MP, Chhattisgarh & Vidarbha Nagpur

68)EXIM Hindi - Textile & Apparel Export

69)EXIM Hindi - Export Import Practical Training In Delhi, Kolkata, Mumbai and Pune

70) Import Export Business

71) Import Export Business Hindi

72) Import Export Business English video

73) Import Export Business Marathi

74) Women in International Business by Exim Guru Adv. JayprakashSomani

75) Opportunities in Foreign Trade- Adv. Jayprakash Somani's special interview

PPP

List Of Adv. Jayprakash Somani's Books

1. Supreme Court of India's Leading Case Laws on 'Insolvency & Bankruptcy Code 2016'

2. Bail Matters – Supreme Court's Latest Leading Case Laws

3. Arbitration Matters- Supreme Court's Latest Leading Case Laws

4. Property Matters - Supreme Court's Latest Leading Case Laws

5. Matrimonial Matters- Supreme Court's Latest Leading Case Laws

6. Election Matters- Supreme Court's Latest Leading Case Laws

7.SEBI Matters- Supreme Court's Latest Leading Case Laws

8. Banking Matters- Supreme Court's Latest Leading Case Laws

9. Service Matters- Supreme Court's Latest Leading Case Laws

10. Contempt of Court Matters- Supreme Court's Latest Leading Case Laws

11. Consumer Protection Matters- Supreme Court's Latest Leading Case Laws

12. Corporate Law- Supreme Court's Latest Leading Case Laws

13. Supreme Court's AOR Exam- Leading Cases

14. Armed Force Tribunal - Supreme Court's Latest Leading Case Laws

15. Acquittal From 376 - Supreme Court's Latest Leading Case Laws

16. Negotiable instrument – Supreme Court's Latest Leading Case Laws

17. Contract Act- Supreme Court's Latest Leading Case Laws

18. Insider trading- Supreme Court's Latest Leading Case Laws

19. Foreign Exchange and Management Act- Supreme Court's Latest Leading Case Laws

20. Income Tax Act- Supreme Court's Latest Leading Case Laws

PPP

These Books are available online at

1. **Notion Press:**https://notionpress.com/author/jayprakash_somani
2. **Amazon:**https://www.amazon.in/s?k=jayprakash+somani
3. **Flipkart:**https://www.flipkart.com/search?q=Jayprakash%20Somani

PPP

9 798885 552059

Printed by Libri Plureos GmbH in Hamburg,
Germany